SUPER POWER MEMORY
for the
Busy Professional

Sushant Mysorekar is trained in educational and career counselling and psychology. He has over fifteen years of experience in training, mentoring and research in the field of Cognition and Intelligence, and has been certified by the Institute of Psychological Health. He has been working with Pharmaceutical, Steel and Ophthalmic industries in various roles in Sales, Marketing, Production and Material and Scrap Procurement. He launched a startup focused on providing training to students and professionals on how to improve their memory by using tools, techniques and systems. Recognized as a 'Gold Medalist Master Trainer' in the Musical Windows Memorization Systems used globally, he is an internationally acclaimed trainer in the field of memory, who has coached students, including students with disabilities, and professionals in more than fifteen countries. He has trained professionals from the varied fields of engineering, medicine, the navy, management, etc. and has conducted training programmes for TCS, Oracle and Parle G, to name a few companies. He has also conducted programmes in around seven universities, both in India and abroad.

He has received the Excellence Award from the Asia-Africa Development Council, India, and the University of Mumbai, for his contributions in the field of education. As the Vice President of Indian Memory Sports Council, India, he promotes and organizes school- and national-level memory championships in India as well as abroad. He is renowned for his counselling skills and memory optimization methods that have helped his students excel in innovation and creativity. His previous book was *Super Tips for Super Memory*.

SUPER POWER MEMORY
for the
Busy Professional

Sushant Mysorekar

RUPA

Published by
Rupa Publications India Pvt. Ltd 2020
7/16, Ansari Road, Daryaganj
New Delhi 110002

Sales Centres:

Allahabad Bengaluru Chennai
Hyderabad Jaipur Kathmandu
Kolkata Mumbai

Copyright © Sushant Mysorekar 2020
Illustrations by Avanti Salwatkar

The views and opinions expressed in this book are the
author's own and the facts are as reported by him which
have been verified to the extent possible, and the publishers
are not in any way liable for the same.

All rights reserved.
No part of this publication may be reproduced, transmitted,
or stored in a retrieval system, in any form or by any means,
electronic, mechanical, photocopying, recording or otherwise,
without the prior permission of the publisher.

ISBN: 978-93-5333-764-3

First impression 2020

10 9 8 7 6 5 4 3 2 1

The moral right of the author has been asserted.

Printed at HT Media Ltd., Gr Noida

This book is sold subject to the condition that it shall not,
by way of trade or otherwise, be lent, resold, hired out, or otherwise
circulated, without the publisher's prior consent, in any form of binding or
cover other than that in which it is published.

Contents

Introduction vii

Chapter 1: First Things First: The Important Questions 1

Chapter 2: Understanding Memory 11

Chapter 3: Creativity at the Workplace 17

Chapter 4: Stories for the Brain 27

Chapter 5: Learning and Working Styles 38

Chapter 6: Handling Successful Meetings and Discussions 48

Chapter 7: The Importance of Connections 54

Chapter 8: Understanding Intelligence 67

Chapter 9: Remembering Appointments 81

Chapter 10: Faster Reading Speed 88

Chapter 11: Creative Thinking 107

Chapter 12: Connecting and Engaging with Customers 117

Chapter 13: Positive Stress 123

Chapter 14: Meditation and Relaxation 130

Chapter 15: Learning a Foreign Language 134

Chapter 16: Tackling Memory Disorders 146

Acknowledgements 157

Introduction

Congratulations! If you have picked up this book, you are one of the amazing people who have taken this powerful first step in understanding today's need for an environment that nurtures their aspirations and visions for the future. This book shall guide you, through a step-by-step process, in the journey to excellence. The tools, techniques and systems used in this book have been designed exclusively to suit twenty-first century needs.

In the course of reading this book, you will learn the principles of using your memory to your optimum benefit. These will be your steps towards success in your professional and personal lives. Learning how to use and implement the techniques will help you effortlessly remember information, which will make your career skyrocket. You can even spare yourself the sheer inconvenience of storing loads of data, information and details of the people you meet.

Learning is a continuous process, and you can start training your memory at any age. Let me elucidate my point with a real-life example of a legend who started doing so at the age of seventy-seven and not only learnt, but also participated in the World Memory Championship and won the gold medal. He is Mr Mahadev Kalokhe from Nashik.

Here is his story in his own words:

> My journey started when I accompanied my grandson to a memory programme arranged in my village. My

grandson did not have any friends there. So, I too joined the programme to help him in case he needed any. Unfortunately he did not enjoy the programme, but I enjoyed it very much. The subject of memory was an altogether new one to me. However, I took up the challenge and started working on it. During this period, I met my mentor Vikrant Chaphekar, who helped me in understanding the techniques better. I worked under his guidance and prepared for the World Memory Championships 2016 held in Singapore. I also received additional techniques and guidance from Sushant Mysorekar sir. I worked for almost two-and-a-half months with complete dedication, for around sixteen to eighteen hours a day. It was a difficult journey, but I simply concentrated on my aim to become a memory champion. Then, finally, with God's grace and my dedication and hard work, I won the medal for India.

Now, we too can emulate Mahadev's story and, if not become a memory champion, can surely train our memory to excel both at work and at home.

However, before we start anything new, we need to analyse our core strengths and risk-taking capabilities and set our short-, mid- and long-term goals.

Individual Introspection

Before we start with detailed information, knowledge and lessons about the brain, we need to first check the understanding/working of our present memory.

If you are not sure how this book can help you, let us go through this assessment test. You can simply tick whichever box is applicable to you and get to know yourself better.

Gender: ☐ Male ☐ Female ☐ Other
Age Group: ☐ 19-25 ☐ 26-59 ☐ 60 and above
(in years)

1. Do I know the useful systems for better performance at work?
   ☐ I need to know ☐ I have some idea ☐ I know
2. Do I have a natural ability to perform certain activities?
   ☐ I need to learn ☐ I have some idea ☐ I know
3. Do I know how I can learn better?
   ☐ I need to know ☐ I have some idea ☐ I know
4. Do I know different ways of solving similar challenges?
   ☐ I need to know ☐ I have some idea ☐ I know
5. Can I recall 80-90 per cent of what I have just read?
   ☐ I need to know ☐ I have some idea ☐ I know
6. Do I know how to read at the speed of 600-800 wpm (words per minute) with 80-90 per cent retention?
   ☐ I need to know ☐ I have some idea ☐ I know
7. Do I know how data/contents can be represented?
   ☐ I need to know ☐ I have some idea ☐ I know
8. Do I know the art of calculating mentally?
   ☐ I need to know ☐ I have some idea ☐ I know
9. Do I know the art of recalling the right information at the right time?
   ☐ I need to know ☐ I have some idea ☐ I know
10. Do I remember what I hear, see or read—directions, peoples' names, travel locations, stories, novels, educational content, etc.?

HEAR ☐ I need to learn ☐ I have some idea ☐ I know
SEE ☐ I need to learn ☐ I have some idea ☐ I know
READ ☐ I need to learn ☐ I have some idea ☐ I know

11. Do I know the art of focused attention?
    ☐ I need to know ☐ I have some idea ☐ I know

12. Do I know the art of communication?
    ☐ I need to know   ☐ I have some idea   ☐ I know
13. Do I know the art of listening to sounds, music, etc. clearly and accurately?
    ☐ I need to know   ☐ I have some idea   ☐ I know
14. Do I know how to remember the names of the people I meet?
    ☐ I need to know   ☐ I have some idea   ☐ I know
15. Do I know how to remember faces?
    ☐ I need to know   ☐ I have some idea   ☐ I know
16. Do I know the art of curiosity?
    ☐ I need to know   ☐ I have some idea   ☐ I know
17. Do I know the thinking- and decision-making process?
    ☐ I need to learn ☐ I have some idea   ☐ I know
18. Have I ever tested myself for creativity?
    ☐ Never   ☐ Sometimes   ☐ Frequently
19. Do I know smart methods to adapt to a corporate environment?
    ☐ I need to know   ☐ I have some idea   ☐ I know
20. Do I know the actual process of learning, unlearning and relearning any concept?
    ☐ I need to know   ☐ I have some idea   ☐ I know

IF YOU HAVE MARKED:

☐ I need to know/learn; it means that you are ready to learn and that you wish to improve on your skills. You are about to take the first step in improving your memory skills.

☐ I have some idea; it means that you are aware about some aspects, but are not sure how they are going to help you. However, you are ready to learn and improve your memory skills.

☐ I know; it means that you are aware of some techniques and

Introduction • xi

systems. You may have learnt them yourself, or undergone a brain development training programme.

This book shall help all professionals, no matter what their profession. Now let us identify the challenges you face while dealing with situations pertaining to your industry and/or profession.

It is imperative that you introspect on certain key areas and check your abilities and learning.

READING

Answer the following questions and introspect on your reading skills.

1. Do you agree that reading is a skill?
   Yes/No
2. How do you read?
   a) Silently.
   b) Aloud.
   c) Using gestures.
3. What do you read?
   a) Newspapers
   b) Magazines
   c) Novels
   d) Reports
   e) Any other literature _____
4. What percentage of a text can you recall after reading it once?
   a) 100 per cent
   b) Between 90-100 per cent
   c) Between 80-90 per cent
   d) Between 70-80 per cent
   e) Less than 70 per cent
5. How many times do you need to read a text to remember

at least 90 per cent of what you have read?
   a) Only once
   b) Two times
   c) Three times
   d) More than three times
6. What are the three main benefits you can achieve if you know how to read?
   a) _____
   b) _____
   c) _____
7. How many books do you read in…?
   a) One month: _____
   b) Three months: _____
   c) Six months: _____
   d) One year: _____
8. What form of books do you prefer reading? (You can select multiple options.)
   a) Non-fiction
   b) Books filled with colour images and symbols
   c) Comics
   d) Fiction
9. You prefer to read on:
   a) Print
   b) Kindle
   c) Mobile
10. Do you like to… (You can select multiple options.)
    a) Read
    b) Listen
    c) Participate (in debates, discussions)
    d) Chat (Whatsapp, Facebook, etc.)

Calculating your reading speed:

1. My reading speed = ___wpm (words per minute)
   Comprehension = ___per cent

If you are not sure how to calculate, follow the instructions below:

Step 1: Place any material with text i.e. (manual/case study/reports) in front of you.

Step 2: Time your reading for two minutes.

Step 3: Start reading the material the way you normally read, and stop reading when you hear the alarm (i.e. after two minutes).

Step 4: Count the number of words read in the two minute duration—let's say 'X' words.

Step 5: Now divide that number 'X' by 2. That gives you your score of 'Y' wpm.

Let's consider, for example, that you have read 200 words in two minutes.

Divide the number by 2. 200 ÷ 2 = 100. **Your reading speed is 100 wpm.**

MEMORY

1. How would you rate your memory?
   a) Excellent
   b) Good
   c) Poor
   d) Very poor
2. Do you think you are creative?
   a) Yes

b) No
3. Do you face difficulty in remembering dates and events?
   a) Yes
   b) No
4. Do you remember the names of the customers/associates/people visiting your office if they meet you again after a week?
   a) Yes
   b) No
5. Can you recall the phone numbers of your family/close friends? (Assume you need to make an urgent call and your mobile is switched off due to low battery.)
   a) Yes
   b) No
6. Can you recall passwords/other important data?
   a) Yes
   b) No
7. Do you tend to become blank or fade out during discussions/meetings?
   a) Yes
   b) No
8. Do you feel that you have excellent memory in certain areas? If yes, what are they?
   a) _____
   b) _____
   c) _____
9. Where do you feel you can improve your memory?
   a) _____
   b) _____
   c) _____
10. What are the top three skills you feel you should have?
    a) _____
    b) _____

c) _____

Does this happen to you?

- You start reading a book, and after reading a few pages, you forget the beginning.
- You learn a new word, and after a few days, you are not able to recollect that particular word.
- You invest your hard-earned money and take an online/offline course, but after some time you hardly remember anything.
- You dial a new number, but after some time, you forget the number altogether.
- You meet someone new for brunch, have a conversation with them for half an hour, and then forget their face or name or both.
- You forget some important event or gift—perhaps your spouse's birthday!

Daily Possible Challenges:

Let us now look at some of the challenges we encounter in our lives.

Tick whichever applies to you.

- ☐ I tend to forget instructions after sometime.
- ☐ I forget some words during discussions.
- ☐ I am unable to concentrate for a long time.
- ☐ I am not so creative.
- ☐ I am not able to manage people.
- ☐ I am unable to recall numbers.
- ☐ I face difficulty in remembering names.
- ☐ I face difficulty in remembering faces.

- ☐ I mostly forget important dates or events.
- ☐ My reading speed is low.

By now, I am sure you understand the importance of training your brain, and are ready to move ahead.

What if this happens suddenly...

- You remember the contents of an entire book.
- You feel appreciated and applauded every time you recall something at the right time.
- You recall the topics, examples and case studies of an online/offline course days after finishing it.
- You are able to recollect contact details, addresses and even minute details about your friends, relatives or colleagues.

Now we must identify the core areas that we need to focus on.

- ☐ Programming our neurons
- ☐ Improving memory habits
- ☐ Improving our level of thinking
- ☐ Improving vocabulary
- ☐ Improving visual intelligence
- ☐ Improving observation skills
- ☐ Improving reading skills
- ☐ Improving concentration skills
- ☐ Improving decision-making skills
- ☐ Developing reading habits
- ☐ Improving innovative strategies
- ☐ Improving creative quotient
- ☐ Improving numerical ability
- ☐ Improving audio skills
- ☐ Improving creative visualization
- ☐ Improving learning habits

Now that you have introspected on different aspects of memory, you have a fairly good idea of what you know and your core skills, as well as the areas that need improvement. My intention in writing this chapter is to make you aware of your inner abilities, sharpen your skills and enhance your performance. You can now move ahead and learn how to improvise on your skills and abilities. We must explore new systems that can not only help you in your professional journey, but also create personal satisfaction.

Summary

In this chapter, we have learnt:

- Introspection
- To calculate reading speed
- Facts about memory

Chapter 1

First Things First: The Important Questions

Introduction

When we conduct seminars, workshops and training programmes, we receive a lot of interesting questions. We all agree that the brain is the most vital organ, which controls the whole mechanism of the body—its movements, senses and actions. Recent studies have shown that with proper tools, you can achieve anything in life. I have compiled the most frequently asked questions, along with my answers. They will hopefully clear your doubts and prepare you to gradually learn the tips and techniques for better memory.

On Memory

Why is it important to have good memory?

Memory is important for us in our day to day lives. Imagine a situation where you have lost your memory. How would you react? How would you respond to situations? How would you take any decision? Our experiences, relationships and emotions are based on facts stored in our memory. A good memory can improve your career, help you take better decisions and decrease your stress level. The better your memory performance, the better will be the quality of your work-life balance.

Does good memory mean high intelligence?

Intelligence is the ability to acquire and apply your knowledge and skills. The key to intelligence is to juggle multiple thoughts, work on mental skills, or recall stored memories at the right time. A good memory can help individuals in varied ways—from complex problem-solving to social intelligence. The sharper your memory skills, the better your quality and quantity of recall at any given time.

What is good or bad memory?

The truth is that there is no such thing as a bad or good memory, only a trained memory and an untrained one. Like anything else, memory is a skill that can be mastered. All you need is an effective method and powerful systems, which are the secrets behind all successful people. You shall be learning these systems, tools and techniques in the chapters ahead. You will soon be among the few who enjoy the benefits of a trained memory.

How does memory work?

There are three major processes involved in memory: encoding, storage and retrieval (decoding).

Every activity we perform throughout the day is recorded in the brain—activities such as travelling, working in an office environment, meeting people, touching a pen, using a mobile phone, tasting food, processing information like listening to the name of a person when they are introduced. This is the first stage—encoding.

The second stage involves storing the information. Sensory memory is the ability to retain impressions of sensory information after the original stimuli have ended, i.e., after a few seconds.

Short-term memory is also called active memory and has the capacity to retain a small amount of information in the mind in an active, readily available state for a short period of time—maybe for a few seconds, minutes, hours or even days. **Long-term memory** is where informative knowledge is held indefinitely. Information that we pay attention to or document with interest, or connect to with emotions, is stored in either short- or long-term memory as per our requirements.

The final stage, i.e. retrieval, is achieved when the retained information needs to be presented at a given time. Recall or retrieval of memory means accessing events or information from the past that have been previously encoded and stored in the brain in the form of emotions, senses, tools, techniques or systems—a process commonly known as remembering.

How is memory stored and then recalled at a later date, even decades later?

Inputs are received through electrical and chemical transmitters in the form of words, emotions, feelings, senses and body movements. Each neuron stores information, and signals are transmitted from one neuron to another. This process of storing information and connections takes place through the synapses that hold them together. Information, feelings or emotions that are important get stored in short-term memory while information that adds value, or requires to be repeated, or can be used later, is stored in long-term memory.

Is it possible to improve memory?

The human brain has an astonishing ability to adapt and change at any age. You can harness the natural power of neuroplasticity, the ability of the brain to change throughout an individual's lifetime, to increase your cognitive abilities, enhance your ability to learn new information, and improve your memory at any age. Eighty-seven-year-old Dr Francis Xavier from Bangalore and seventy-eight-year-old Mahadev Kalokhe from Nashik are living examples of senior individuals who have made marks in the field of memory.

On the Human Brain

What are a human brain's functions?

The brain is an important organ in the human body. It is made up of a large mass of nerve tissue within the skull. The brain controls our thoughts, memories, speech, movement of arms and legs, etc. It processes sensory information, regulates blood pressure and breathing, and controls the smooth functioning of many organs within our body.

How can we memorize large amounts of information?

The potential of the human brain is unlimited. But we have not been taught how to read information, understand it, store it and reproduce it later. By learning different techniques and systems, we can grasp the process of learning, reading, memorizing and recalling information. The following chapters will teach you the techniques of memorizing large amounts of data easily.

Albert Einstein used 10 per cent of the brain. Is this a myth or a fact?

It is a widely spread myth that most or all humans only use 10 per cent (or some other small percentage) of their brains. It has been misattributed to many people, including Albert Einstein.

Researchers show that most of the brain is in use most of the time, even when a person is performing a very simple action. A large part of the brain is even active when a person is resting or sleeping.

The percentage of the brain in use at any given time varies from person to person. It also depends on what a person is doing or thinking about.

Do people lose brain cells?

We naturally lose brain cells, but with every new activity we perform, we make new connections and activate cells. We may lose some nerve connections as we grow older. It can be part of the redesigning of the brain that occurs with experience. It's possible that we can even grow and strengthen our brain cells through exercises, puzzles, new activities or tasks, etc. With every new activity, we create new connections, and with regular practice, we strengthen them.

Is it true that whatever I have learnt is locked in my brain, and I just need the right key to unlock it?

No, our memories are not locked, but they are constantly rearranged, shuffled or remoulded. Whatever we learn with interest, purpose and a goal in mind is registered in memory and stored. This stored information creates patterns and the more we practice or reiterate it, the more we are able to master the patterns. We forget selectively too, since even if the key to the information is right, the room you step in may have been remodelled.

Which part of the brain controls memory?

The hippocampus is a structure in the brain that has been associated with various memory functions. It is part of the limbic system, and lies next to the medial temporal lobe.

Which part of the brain is responsible for learning?

The cerebrum, the large outer part of the brain, controls reading, thinking, learning, speech, emotions and planned muscle movements like walking. It also controls vision, hearing and other senses.

Can brain cells be reproduced?

Brain cells are complicated structures, with spider-like tentacles. For a very long time, researchers believed that the number of brain cells you were born with was a predetermined amount—that you could certainly lose some cells due to old age, brain damage, etc., but you couldn't get any more. In 1965, a scientist named Joseph Altma claimed to have evidence to the contrary. He proposed a process called 'neurogenesis' or generation of neurons. Since then it has been proved that brain cells can be reproduced, but only in specific areas of the brain—some of them being the cerebral cortex or the outer layer of the brain; the cerebellum or the back of the brain, which is important for motor control and the olfactory area, important for processing smell.

What is 'neurogenesis' for?

Now, most neurogenesis happens in the hippocampus—important for learning and memory. So a constant flow of new brain cells is necessary for learning and memory. New neurons can be integrated into existing connections, which allows for new memories without interrupting old ones. New cells can also be a way to separate overlapping memories.

On Intelligence Quotient (IQ)

What is considered to be a good IQ score?

On many tests, a score of 100 is considered the average IQ. 68 per cent of scores fall within one standard, i.e., between 85 and 115. It means that nearly 70 per cent of all people score within ± 15 points of the average score.

Can IQ be learnt?

Yes, your IQ can change over time. But IQ tests taken over a period of a year show little variation in their results. The older you are, the more stable your test score will be. IQ scores are most volatile during childhood and ad olescence. If a child works on their weak areas and practices key situations, they can perform better and get an overall superior IQ score.

Can anyone become a genius?

Yes, it is true that anyone can become a genius, but it takes a lot of dedication and focus. With proper training, the right environment, the right tools and techniques and consistent practice, anyone can achieve excellence.

On Sleep

Why do we need to sleep?

Sleep helps our body to relax and our brain to develop and grow. We sleep in order to regenerate the damaged parts of our body. Researchers have also shown that after a person sleeps, they tend to retain information and perform better on memory tasks. Our body needs rest, and it does so through sleep. It also helps to grow muscles, repair tissue and synthesize hormones.

Which part of the brain is responsible for dreams?

Dreams are basically stories and images that our mind creates while we sleep. Dreams can be vivid. They can occur anytime during sleep. But most vivid dreams occur during deep REM (rapid eye movement) sleep, when the brain is most active. Dreaming is unilateral—i.e., mostly only one side of the brain is functioning at any given time while you are asleep. Studies have shown that this stage of sleep helps the brain connect unrelated ideas, which, in turn, aids creative problem-solving.

Is sleep related to memory?

Both registration and recall are functions that take place when your brain, mind and body are awake. However, researchers believe that sleep is required for consolidation of memory, no matter the memory type (sensory, short- or long-term memory). Without adequate sleep, your brain has a harder time absorbing and recalling new information. Sleep does more than help sharpen the mind.

What makes dreams possible and from where do we get those ideas, stories etc. while sleeping?

Dreams are hallucinations that occur during certain stages of sleep. The creative brain i.e., the right brain takes over all operations while we sleep. The logical brain, which is active throughout the day, needs rest and hence gets inactive during sleep. This is how it makes time for repairs. The creative brain takes over from the logical brain, thus creating virtual experiences. While dreaming, the brain also refreshes stored memories and creates these virtual experiences of joy, sorrow and sometimes fear from what we see, experience and think during the day—but it is not a rule.

On Memory Loss

What causes memory loss or forgetfulness?

Memory loss or forgetfulness is a natural phenomenon. Many people worry about being forgetful. We must remember here that we cannot forget events we do not register. Let's say we meet a new person and then exchange cards/names. How many of us will recall the other person's name after some time? We did not register the name at the first instance, and so inactiveness caused forgetfulness.

Other causes for memory problems can include ageing, medical conditions, emotional problems, mild cognitive impairment or dementia.

Can memory be restored?

For decades, most neuroscientists have believed that memories are stored at the synapses—the connections between brain cells, or neurons. When the connection is lost, the information stored is lost. If you can restore the synaptic connections, the memory will come back. It can be achieved with certain techniques, regular brain exercises and consistent practice. You can find these techniques and several exercises in the chapters ahead.

How can I reduce memory loss?

First and foremost, to improve memory, you need to be consciously aware of what you are doing, and stay mentally active. Secondly, get organized before you plan any activity. Create a schedule or a to-do list and follow the instructions well. Thirdly, do not multitask. Our brain is not designed for multitasking. Do one thing at a time.

Regular exercise and meditation can help you to keep your brain cells active. Reading, writing, solving puzzles, discussions and debates are some of the other ways you can keep your brain healthy.

Summary

In this chapter, we have addressed frequently asked questions on:

- Memory
- The human brain
- Sleep
- Memory loss

Chapter 2

Understanding Memory

Introduction

Memory is nothing but a storage space, where all information and data related to your past experiences, emotions, feelings, exchange of words and incidents are stored, so that when in need, we can just search and find the relevant information as quickly as possible.

Sensory memory stores the information for a few seconds before it is lost. If the information is repeated, it gets stored in **short-term memory**. If the person is important for business or in sync with our likes and dislikes, we feel that they are important to us. Therefore, we retain information such as their manner of speech, style, dressing and presentation, as well as their credentials, relationships, references, etc., and store all of it in **long-term memory**. This information can be retrieved and used hours, days, months or even years later.

How do we each have our own individual personalities and traits?

Our individual habits, behaviours, feelings and emotions create a pattern of how we deal with or reciprocate to the people we meet. Our personal way of expression creates an impression of us—whether we are warm or cold, respectful or rude, polite or arrogant, and so on.

Memory could be compared to a library or the records storage room of a large corporation. Memories are stored in specific brain cells. By triggering a small cluster of neurons, researchers have been able to force the body to recall a specific memory. By removing these neurons, the body would lose that memory.

Let us understand the brain and the various aspects of memory.

Types of Memory

Sensory memory holds sensory information for less than a second after something is perceived by the mind. When you look at something very quickly, say, for a split second, and briefly remember what it looked like, it is an example of sensory memory. If this information is passed on to short-term memory, it will be retained for a longer period of time.

We regularly visit different places and register a large amount of information subconsciously. When we are asked about any of these locations, the things we instantly remember are the ones that are stored in sensory memory.

For example: When you meet someone for the first time and share your respective names and other details, you only retain that information for a short time before it is lost. You can recall their face, as visual information is stored in the occipital lobe, but the information that has not been stored, i.e. the name, is lost.

Working memory or short-term memory (or 'primary' or 'active memory') is the capacity to keep a small amount of information in the mind in a readily available manner for a short time. For example, you can use your short-term memory to remember a phone number that you have just called. The duration of short-term memory is only a few seconds or minutes.

For example: When you receive oral instructions from your boss, or when you are simultaneously talking on the phone while listening to a list of groceries to be bought, you will most likely retain the information in your short-term memory for only a brief period of time unless you note it down.

Long-term memory is when informative knowledge is retained in the mind indefinitely. Long-term memory can store a large amount of information for an unlimited period of time (sometimes a complete life span). For example, if we are given a random six-digit number, we may remember it for only a few seconds because it was stored in our short-term memory. However, if the same number is repeated regularly, you will remember it for a much longer duration, maybe even a lifetime.

Examples of long-term memory include recollection of important days from the past such as birthdays, anniversaries, important events, etc., and work skills that you learn in your professional life.

Topographic memory is our capacity to orient ourselves in specific environments or recognize places that we are familiar with. Our topographic memory is weak when, for instance, we get lost while travelling alone. Sharp topographic memory includes clear spatial/visual images and the ability to recall these images or locations.

A **flashbulb memory** is a clear, episodic memory of an event that has left a deep, emotional impact.

For example, there are people who remember where they were or what they were doing when they first received the news of a major accident involving a huge loss, or heard of some catastrophe or natural calamity. In such instances, people exercise their flashbulb memory.

Declarative memory, also referred to as explicit memory, involves consciously remembering or recalling facts, dates and events.

Declarative memory can be further sub-divided into semantic memory, which concerns general principles and facts, and episodic memory, which is contextual.

Procedural memory (or implicit memory) is the opposite of declarative memory and is based on implicit learning rather than recalling information through conscious effort. It is the memory that is used to learn and retain motor skills. When we become better at something only by doing it over and over again, we are employing procedural memory.

Examples of procedural memory are riding a bicycle, following workplace rules or systems, preparing tea or coffee, etc.

Autobiographical memory is a system of memory that consists of episodes remembered from an individual's life. It is a mix of personal experiences, such as things, people and events we have come across in life, associated with specific contexts (episodic memory), and generic information about the world (semantic memory).

Activity

Please proceed with the questions below and answer 'Yes' or 'No'.

1. I am confident while speaking with my seniors/boss.
   _____
   _____

2. I can express my feelings in front of others.
   _____
   _____

3. I can systematically explain processes to my subordinates.

4. I can recall experiences and can narrate them as they were.

5. I am capable of performing tasks in stipulated time frames.

6. I can speak confidently in group situations.

7. I can remember roads that I have travelled on just once.

8. I can handle my appointments.

9. I can handle presentations.

10. I can speak on any topic at the spur of the moment.

If your answers are mostly 'yes', that means that you have a good memory for names which, in turn, can help you develop a good working relationship with your client, making you more comfortable in meetings or in social gatherings. If your answers are mostly 'no', it means that you face challenges while recalling either names or other information.

Summary

In this chapter, we have learnt:

- How memory works
- How memory is stored
- Why we dream
- Why we sleep
- What makes us who we are
- Memory as a function of the mind
- Types of memory

Chapter 3

Creativity at the Workplace

Introduction

In today's world, creativity is recognized as a practical skill rather than something reserved for artists or geniuses. Creativity is no longer about thinking out of the box, but more a skill that anyone can learn and apply in their professional and personal lives.

It is a way of thinking, where we look at familiar things with new eyes, examining a particular problem with an open mind and developing a different perspective on how it might be solved. We use our imagination, along with our knowledge, experiences and learning, to explore new possibilities rather than the old and established methods.

The Importance of Creativity

Creativity is a basic necessity for you to form opinions and express your views for your personal and professional growth, innovation and development. There is no doubt that it is the key that can open your mind to make you learn better, understand what you have learnt and remember it well. Pupils who are encouraged to think creatively have improved self-esteem, better motivation, achieve more and are lively and spontaneous.

Creative people...

- become more interested in discovering new things for themselves
- are more open to new ideas and challenges
- are better at solving problems
- can work well with others
- become more effective learners

The challenge for professionals is to nourish and develop the natural creativity in people, and not stifle it.

Approaches That Can Help You Nurture Your Creativity

- Find regular opportunities for hands-on activities, problem-solving, discussions and collaborative work.
- Actively try at all levels to question things, make connections, note all possible outcomes and explore innovative ideas.
- Look at case studies of failures or setbacks as opportunities to learn from mistakes.
- Have open discussions/brainstorm about key challenging areas that you, as a professional, are facing and how you can solve them.
- Ask open-ended questions such as 'What if...?', 'How differently...', and 'How to?' to make your brain think in varied ways.

Activity

Resource(s) required: A small pocket notebook
Process: First, make a list of some relevant topics such as 'how to reduce the use of plastic'. Then note down your ideas in a small pocket 'idea book'.

TOPIC_____Idea 1: _____
TOPIC_____Idea 2: _____
TOPIC_____Idea 3: _____
TOPIC_____Idea 4: _____
TOPIC_____Idea 5: _____

Sometimes we tend to have self-doubt and do not attempt any creative challenges. The mental blocks that prevent creative activity are:

a) I am not very creative.
b) I strictly follow rules and regulations.
c) There is a right answer for everything.
d) This doesn't seem to be logical.
e) I am very practical in my approach.
f) I don't want to make any mistakes.
g) Creative people are all mad.
h) I don't want to waste my time with frivolous things.

Phrases That Kill Creativity

1. 'It's too much work.'
2. 'It hasn't been done before.'
3. 'Get your head out of the clouds.'
4. 'Yeah. We've tried that before.'
5. 'You have a point, but…'
6. 'It costs too much.'
7. 'That isn't your problem.'
8. 'We don't have time.'
9. 'Good idea, but it's impractical.'
10. 'Stay in your place.'
11. 'You are ahead of time.'
12. 'It's too radical.'

13. 'You can't teach an old dog new tricks.'
14. 'It won't work.'
15. 'We have always done it this way.'

Can we change the above statements using a creative approach?

1. Let us work in phases and celebrate small successes.
2. Let us check what happens; perhaps we might get some new perspective.
3. Let us put our heads together to generate new and fresh ideas.
4. Let us try with a different approach.
5. You have a point; can I add something to it?
6. Let us first focus on the idea and check if we can save on cost later.
7. Can we see the problem from all angles?
8. Let us find someone to work on this idea.
9. Good idea; can you please shed more light and check if it's practical?
10. Open your mind and let your thoughts flow.
11. Wow! Can we mould this idea to see if it is applicable today?
12. Can we rethink on these lines?
13. Let us take a chance to change the old logic and apply a new perspective.
14. Let us consider this for now and check if it is applicable with time.
15. Let us change this time and try something new!

Activity

Alphabet pictures

Process: Develop a creative touch and stimulate your brain.

Creativity at the Workplace • 21

Just check the shape, say, for example, 'A'. Now create an object or animal using the shape of the alphabet as shown in the example below.

Similarly design your own shapes and create images from your memory for the remaining letters.

A	B	C	D	E
F	G	H	I	J
			K	L
M	N	O	P	Q
R	S	T	U	V
W	X	Y	Z	

Some of the Steps to Enhance Your Creative Process:

- Compare and combine: Mentally rearrange and connect ideas, thoughts and objects to create a new thought process that can spark and register new learnings. This is explained in detail in later chapters.
- Risk-taking: Every business enterprise needs to think differently.
- Ask 'How?' and 'What if?'
- Transform your viewpoint.
- Visit other places.
- Incubate.
- Trigger concepts.

Here Are Some Daily Doses of Creativity:

- Explore new routes.
- Start something new every day.
- Close your eyes and visualize an object—say an apple. Consider the object from all angles.
- Connect one object to another and create a weird mental image. For example, connect your watch with your office chair and try to imagine the chair moving in a clockwise direction as time passes.

Activity

Resource(s) required: A small pocket notebook

Topic for discussion: If your organization appoints you as a CEO for one day, what are the things that you would like to change?

Process: Note down your ideas in the small pocket 'innovation' book.

Think of instant solutions using your gut feeling/intuition.

Idea #1	Idea #2	Idea #3	Idea #4	Idea #5
Idea #6	Idea #7	Idea #8	Idea #9	Idea #10

The Disney Method

Developed in 1994 by Robert Dilts as a model based on the creative process of the legendary Walt Disney, the strategy known as the Disney Method uses four different, successive thinking styles to creatively deal with challenges. Through these four styles—outsiders, dreamers, realizers and critics—the method seeks to creatively and constructively analyze problems and develop plans of action.

The ten beliefs at the heart of the Disney Method:[1]

1. Give every member of your organization a chance to dream, and tap into the creativity embodied by those dreams.
2. Stand firm on your beliefs and principles.
3. Treat you customers like beloved guests.
4. Trust, support, empower and appreciate your employees with rewards.
5. Build and maintain long-term relationships with suppliers and partners.
6. Dare to innovate and take calculated risks for successful implementation.

---

[1] http://braindancingsmorgasbord.blogspot.com/2009/07/

7. Align employees' and associates' views with the company's culture and ethics.
8. Use the storyboarding technique (display your ideas in a sequence) to solve planning and communication problems.
9. Pay close attention to detail and encourage others.
10. Make individuals a part of the journey to success. Let them feel it.

Activity

Question persistently. Ask 'why', 'what if', 'why not', and other such questions—the more (seemingly) ridiculous the question is, the better.

What if you allow your family members to play roles in the office?
   Thoughts about what roles you shall offer:

___

What if you design a room for dreaming?
   Ideas on what that room should look like:

___

Imagine if you could travel round the world!
   Thoughts on the places you would like to visit:

___

Imagine if you found a way to boost your memory 100 per cent!
   Thoughts on how it would change your professional career:

___

A Road Map to Creativity:

- Pay attention to small bursts of thoughts, as they may actually be stunning ideas.
- Daydream! Let your mind wander.
- Indulge yourself! Try out diverse things and enjoy yourself. Here is your creativity schedule for the week.
  Monday: Cooking
  Tuesday: Drawing and painting
  Wednesday: Photography
  Thursday: Writing
  Friday: Trying to make new things
  Saturday: Playing squash, chess
  Sunday: Dancing
- Maintain a 'creativity' file. Record and celebrate your successes. Consciously strive to be creative every day.
- Learn a foreign language (and force your brain to think in multiple ways, improve your accent, style and create new patterns to learn the words).
- Cultivate ambidexterity—try to use both your right and left hands equally well. Develop coordination. If you're right-handed, try using your left hand to do things. If you're left-handed, switch to your right for a while.

Activity

Visit a garden and sit quietly for a few minutes. Observe your surroundings and then close your eyes and imagine how you wish to see the garden. What changes would you like to see? Note it down in your diary.

Visual:	Sound:
Feel:	Smells:
Touch:	Hear:

Now, here are some concrete suggestions for enhancing creativity at the workplace:

1. Schedule meetings only if necessary.
2. Set aside office time for discussions on innovative topics.
3. Don't bother about results; focus on the task in hand.
4. Reduce the time stressing on unimportant issues.
5. Align everyone with the corporate vision.
6. Remain stable yet flexible to changing circumstances.

Summary

In this chapter, we have learnt:

- To understand creativity
- The importance of creativity
- Approaches to promote creativity
- A daily creative routine/dosage
- Phrases that kill creativity
- The ten beliefs at the heart of the Disney Method
- A roadmap to creativity
- Suggestions for the workplace

Chapter 4

Stories for the Brain

Introduction

Our brain develops new connections for every new activity we enact or perform. The information flows from one neuron to another through these connections. Research says that we can connect around 50,000 cells to one cell in many different permutations and combinations. Let's understand what that means.

Let's say you have visited a client's location for a meeting. If you then have to generate Minutes of the Meeting (MOM), recording each and every activity or discussion that took place—who said what, what was accepted and what was rejected, or any little thing that you observed during your stay—you will depend on your brain's record of this information, which is stored in different compartments and recalled when needed.

Let's do an activity to understand what connections our brain has stored and how our mind can help us in retrieving the information:

Activity: Connections in the Brain

Think of any meeting/conference/get together/picnic that you went to.

Now write down what you observed during the event. Write a minimum of ten sentences.

Research says that every human is able to recall around seven items with ease, but as soon as this number exceeds seven, remembering gets difficult. This is where we need to learn some new techniques.

Let's understand the technique of creating a story that is brain-friendly.

The basic rule that we must remember is that the story must fall into at least one of the following categories:

- Memorable
- Unique
- Linked to some important object/event

Now let's start with a story:

1. Create a story: Our brain loves stories, as they help improve its ability to understand and recall. Our brain sees information in terms of images 85 per cent of the time.

    For instance, if we ask you to imagine a bird or an animal of your choice, it is most likely that you'll imagine a picture of the bird or animal in your mind and not its name as a word. From this, it is clear that it is easier to remember any

object or place by its image than by its name or spelling.
2. A story should have a link. You need to have a link between each word so that they are all in order and can be memorized sequentially. Link only two words at a time i.e. meeting with presentation and presentation with conference, and so on.
3. Your story should be bizarre. A vivid, abstract, funny, attractive story appeals to our brain and can capture it easily.

The images should be absurd—in a manner that would be difficult to believe in a normal, real-life situation. In short, it should be difficult for your mind to accept. For example, say you imagine yourself holding a zigzag-shaped building on a finger in your right hand. This is absurd and impossible. Our brain accepts such images as food for thought, and hence, they are easy to distinguish and remember.

For example, let's connect the two words 'meeting' and 'presentation'.

A Simple Story: During a meeting, a presentation is being shown.

A Bizarre Story: Close your eyes and visualize a meeting where all the members are sitting together and each person is raising their voice and presenting their views, almost fighting to make themselves heard.

Now which story appeals to you more? The two words, 'meeting' and 'presentation', are now connected through images playing in front of your eyes, completely transformed into a weird story through the use of emotions, style, sound and action.

Note: Rules 1, 2 and 3 are Mandatory.

4. Colours play an important role in our life. Some colours are attractive, some are dull and some are close to our heart.

The use of coloured images in our memory helps us recall objects when required.

For example, consider the words 'presentation' and 'conference'.

Visualize the different bright and shiny colours on each slide of a presentation in a conference room with its distinct smell/fragrance.

Multiple colours mixed together to form a single image or multiple images will help your brain register the concept of the presentation. It also makes for a feel-good effect.

5. Expand or shrink: Mentally expanding or shrinking an object to its highest or lowest possible size, respectively, can light the neurons of your brain. For example, if I tell you to imagine an elephant and you then imagine a tiny elephant walking the streets, it shall help you identify the image immediately.

6. Senses play a very important role: Our eyes are for vision, ears for hearing, nose for smelling, tongue for speech and tasting, and skin for touching. The more your senses are involved in creating a story, the greater are the possibilities of memorization and recall, since your sensory perceptions and consequent emotions are also attached to it.

Let's try to connect 'Virtual Reality (VR)' and a product catalogue. Apply all your senses—visualize a movie in VR that is listed in a product catalogue and is displayed on a screen. Hear the sound too.

7. Emotions such as happiness, sadness, anger, etc. affect the remembrance of an event and help recall it.

For example, let's connect the words 'paying guest (PG)' and 'manage'.

The paying guest staying at your house is angry because there is no water. You are managing the water supply.

8. 2D/3D images: The more dimensions you envision or create, the easier it becomes to link and visualize something.

    For example, let's connect the words 'manage' and 'rehearsal'.

    While managing actors, you find that some well-known film stars are rehearsing for their latest movie and the road to your venue is blocked, preventing you from proceeding.
9. Your presence: Mentally, you can make yourself present at any moment and at any linked point. It is easier to recall an object/person/place that you are directly associated with.

    For example, let's link the words 'rehearsal' and 'file'.

    You are participating in the rehearsal of a play as the lead character. Your job is to design colourful files, and then tear them into pieces and throw them away.
10. Dialogues: Add funny dialogues to make the story interesting and for you to remember it easily.

    For example, let's connect the words 'file' and 'resource'.

    Funny, catchy or famous dialogues play a very important role in connecting stories as they are in easy recall. Analyzing what a particular object may say at a particular moment based on your experience, and visualizing scenes accordingly, has the right impact. For example, imagine a talking file, which moves from one resource person to another, from one table to another.
11. Life: Insert life into lifeless objects as you create and visualize the story. Exercise your imagination and add or modify the values and capabilities of the object.

    For example: Let's connect the words 'resource' and 'salary'.

    Insert life into your salary. It shall visit on its own wherever it wishes, and purchase whatever it requires.

Note: The above points should be applied for two consecutive words at a time in the complete sequence of words, i.e., to connect the first word with the second, the second with the third, and so on—two words at a time only. One should disconnect the first word mentally while associating the second with the third, and so on, as the connections remain intact when you connect only two to three words.

When you connect two images, your brain creates a pattern of neurons. The connection points are called synapses. When you perform the exercises, you need to fix the images in less than six seconds. The key to fast connections is *practise*!

Alternatively, to make it easier, we have also created a simpler format to boost your recall and help you remember what you learnt.

SABCINEMAS

Here, each letter stands for one kind of connection, and a couple of letters for two kinds of connections that our brain can make.

Story: Our brain loves to create stories, which help our neurons to connect with other neurons via a link/bridge called 'synapse'.

Association: If we associate one thing with another, it helps us recall better, because our memories are full of associations and links.

Bizzare: If the associations are generic, our brain stores them for only a short period of time, but if they are unusual, vivid, funny, illogical and different, they can be held for a longer period of time.

Colourful: Our texts are normally in one colour i.e., blue or black, or a combination of the two. Making a text more colourful helps to add value to what we are reading. Colourful images play an important role in remembrance.

Information: The more we know about a certain thing, the more backup information we have to recall important keywords.

New: We all love having new things because the brain loves perceiving new things after periodic gaps. Every new thing we do or perceive creates patterns in our brain.

Expand: Our imagination allows us to freely expand and shrink an object, and that makes it funnier and easier to recall.

Emotions: Our emotions play an important role in connecting us with objects, people, places, etc.

Multiple: The more we imagine things in multiples rather than piecemeal, the better we tend to remember and store information for a longer time.

Multidimensional: We human beings have the power to visualize in multidimensional modes and create multiple patterns in our brains.

All senses: We use our senses to identify multiple things.

Symbols: Symbols help us to connect with the right words. Images speak better and faster than words.

Use the above system, and we assure you that your brain will work faster and remember more easily.

Tips for Creating a Story

- Use positive, pleasant images. Your brain often blocks out unpleasant ones.
- Use vivid, colourful, sensible images—these are easier to remember.
- Use all your senses to code information or dress up an image.

Remember that your pattern of association can contain sounds, smells, tastes, touch, movements and feelings, as well as pictures.
- Give your image three-dimensional movement and space to make it more vivid. You can use movement either to maintain the flow of association, or to help you remember actions.
- Exaggerate the size of the image.
- Use humour! Funny or peculiar things are easier to remember than normal ones.
- Similarly, rude rhymes are very difficult to forget!
- Symbols (red traffic lights, pointing fingers, road signs, etc.) can code quite complex messages quickly and effectively. This means that symbols are self-explanatory and can convey meaning very effectively.

Now let us apply the rules for:

- Recalling minutes of a meeting
- Memorizing discussions during debates/presentations
- Recalling daily activities

Activity

Note down the minutes of your meeting.

_____

_____

_____

_____

_____

Let's now look at the 'location' method of memory:

We tend to use regular routes to travel and have fixed objects at our workplace or residence. These can be ways to recall different activities that we wish to remember from our meetings or presentations or even discussions.

The location system is the concept of connecting the known with the unknown. It means that the objects at our workplace or residence, starting from the 'door,' are known, whereas the information we associate with them is new and unknown, but consequently, easier to remember.

Activity

List the fixed objects in your hall in a sequential order.

For example, before you enter your hall, your first point (we will call each object as a point here to make it simple) of contact is your

Doorbell (then) Door…and so on.

Now, note down the points below, taking into consideration that you start noting points from the right to the left side of your hall:

1. Doorbell	2. Main door	3. _____
4. _____	5. _____	6. _____
7. _____	8. _____	9. _____
10. _____	11. _____	12. _____
13. _____	14. _____	15. _____
16. _____	17. _____	18. _____
19. _____	20. _____	21. _____
22. _____	23. _____	24. _____
25. _____		

Now all the above points are known to you in a sequence. You are also aware of what's before and after each point.

Let's assume that you wish to make a presentation at your workplace, in front of your associates, without looking at the screen. Can you do it? Have you tried this before? If not, let's do it now.

Activity

List the main points of each slide below:

1. Company introduction	2. Vision	3. _____
4. _____	5. _____	6. _____
7. _____	8. _____	9. _____
10. _____	11. _____	12. _____
13. _____	14. _____	15. _____
16. _____	17. _____	18. _____
19. _____	20. _____	21. _____
22. _____	23. _____	24. _____
25. _____		

Now both the 'known' (fixed objects in a sequence) and the 'unknown' (the heading of each slide) have been put up. Connect each element in the 'known' list with its equivalent numbered element in the 'unknown' list by creating a story around each pair.

Now let's apply all the rules we learnt above and check for ourselves if we can give a presentation without looking at the slides. Don't forget to write your feedback below.

_____
_____
_____

Activity

Activate your curiosity and imagination and fire up your ideas to create a suitable story, as we learnt in the previous section.

1. Pick up any magazine. Find the photos in the magazine. Look at them and create a story around them.
2. Switch your television set on. Now mute the sound and try to guess what the people are saying. Create your own story.

Summary

In this chapter, we have learnt:

- To note important points and memorize them
- Nine rules for effective recall
- Tips for creating stories
- Using locations to recall information

Chapter 5

Learning and Working Styles

Introduction

We all have our own styles of learning a particular activity. We develop our habits and behaviours based on our upbringing. Our work is dependent on relevant situations, attachments, feelings and emotions.

There are five types of learning and working styles.[1]

Assessment for Identifying Your Learning Style

Process: Read the questions, try to understand them and attempt to answer them with sincerity.

Sr. No	Details	A	B	C
1	While operating new equipment I prefer to	read the instructions.	listen or ask.	learn by 'trial and error'.
2	For travel directions,	I prefer to carry a map.	I ask for directions.	I follow a compass.
3	While cooking a new dish,	I follow the recipe.	I ask a friend for instructions.	I taste as I cook.

---

[1] https://www.mindtools.com/mnemlsty.html

4	To explain something to someone,	I write down the instructions.	I explain verbally.	I demonstrate.
5	I tend to say,	'I see what you mean.'	'I hear what you say.'	'I know how you feel.'
6	I tend to say,	'Show me.'	'Tell me.'	'Let me try.'
7	I tend to say,	'Watch how I do it.'	'Listen to me explain.'	'You have a go at it.'
8	I prefer these leisure activities:	Museums, galleries, visual scenes.	Music, concerts or plays.	Physical or do-it-yourself activities.
9	While shopping, I generally tend to	look and decide.	discuss with the store staff.	try on, handle or test.
10	To learn a new skill,	I watch someone else doing it.	I try to understand exactly what I am supposed to do.	I like to give it a try and work it out as I go along.
11	While choosing from a restaurant menu,	I imagine what the food will look like.	I go through the options in my head.	I imagine what the food will taste like.
12	When I am listening to a band	I sing along to the lyrics (in my mind!).	I closely listen to the lyrics and the beats.	I move my body in sync with the music.
13	While trying to concentrate,	I focus on the words or pictures in front of me.	I discuss the problem and possible solutions in my mind.	I move around a lot, fiddle with objects in my hand.
14	I remember things best by	writing notes or keeping printed details.	saying them aloud.	doing and practising.
15	My first memory is of	looking at something.	being spoken to.	doing something.
16	When I am anxious,	I visualize the worst-case scenarios.	I talk to myself about what worries me the most.	I can't sit still and fiddle and move around constantly.
17	My first impression about others is formed by	how they look.	what they say.	how they make me feel.

18	When I read reports or journals,	I write design notes (using colours!)	I read them aloud.	I make movements and actions.
19	While expressing my views to friends,	I use various facial expressions.	I use a lot of related jargon.	I use hand gestures.
20	Most of my free time is spent	watching, visualizing, daydreaming.	reading, discussing, debating.	being involved in activities.

Score:

Count the number of times you have marked A, B and C.

Note down the numbers in the boxes given below:

A ☐   B ☐   C ☐

Now let us analyze your answers.

If you chose mostly A's, you have VISUAL learning style.

If you chose mostly B's, you have AUDITORY learning style.

If you chose mostly C's, you have KINESTHETIC learning style.

When you have identified your learning style(s), read the learning styles' explanations below and consider how this might help you identify methods of learning and development that best meet your preference(s).

Visual Learners

Visual learners are those learners who visualize images or pictures.

Qualities of a visual learner:

- Visual learners learn best by visualizing.

- They enjoy connecting with visual scenes.
- They enjoy relating with colour codes.
- They notice visual effects in movies.
- They enjoy watching presentations.
- They follow written instructions and directions.
- They think and prepare themselves well in advance.
- They are good at reading and understanding.
- They can remember faces most prominently.

They can do better in:

- Creating a pictorial representation
- Reading notes, case studies and journals and reproducing them
- Creating an outline of the text
- Making visual maps of targets and achievements

The issues faced by such learners are:

- Having immediate responses to certain ideas
- Designing a faulty layout, if the concept is not understood properly
- Interacting with other types of learners (audio, especially)
- Paying attention to long discussions or long technical meetings

Activity

1. Think of any immediate problem to be resolved. Close your eyes and visualize probable solutions and note them down below.
   Problem area
   _____

Probable solutions

_____
_____
_____

2. Make visual interpretations to express ideas.
   For example:
   Your company's vision for you:

   _____
   _____
   _____

   How will you accomplish your target?
   Your story idea:

3. Create your own dictionary of symbols to represent your ideas (the key points you regularly come across).
   This exercise shall trigger your creative neurons and make them more active when the need arises. It shall also benefit you by helping you note important points in a much faster and more presentable way.

Meetings:	Idea:	_____
Targets:	Assembly line:	_____
Learnings:	Urgent:	_____
Technology:	Follow-up:	_____

4. Solve jigsaw puzzles, Rubik's cubes, mazes or other visual puzzles.

5. Learn to juggle: Juggling makes you **smarter**. It has been proven to enhance your grey matter. Research also suggests it may prevent certain types of brain disease. When you juggle, you exercise your body as well as your mind. In fact, the longer it takes you to learn how to juggle, the more you are exercising your mind!

   Juggling also sharpens your **focus** and **concentration**. The intense focus required for juggling can filter to other areas of your life that need the same kind of close attention.

   Juggling helps you with your **problem-solving skills**.

   Juggling relieves **stress**. While doing the activity, you are so engrossed that it is almost impossible to think of anything else. This helps to escape from things that worry you. It releases the tension and helps you gain clarity and focus.

   Juggling is one of the best ways to improve your coordination.

Important tips:

- Use visual images to recall points.
- Write down clear instructions.
- One on one discussions are preferable for clear idea generation.
- Creative drawings or maps are much easy to understand.
- Observe closely with complete clarity and focus.

Auditory Learners

Qualities of auditory learners:

- Auditory learners learn best by listening consciously.
- They like to read out loud and listen to their own voice.
- They are good at explaining concepts, directions, etc.

- They enjoy listening to audio sessions.
- They follow spoken directions clearly.
- They can call out names easily.
- They notice sound effects in video presentations.
- They like listening to audio in silent environments.
- They are quick in responding to mailers.
- They are good at oral communication.
- They are skilled at speeches or presentations.
- They handle meetings effectively.

The issues faced by such learners are:

- Completing the task at hand
- Visualizing the end result
- Showing directions

Activity

1. Listen to audio files.
2. Read out reports loudly in your mind.
3. Spend one hour listening to unfamiliar styles of music.
4. Play the keyboard and learn simple melodies.
5. Learn to identify different sounds.
6. Write in your dairy daily.

Important tips

- Use word association to remember facts and points.
- Provide both oral and written instructions.
- Watching audio-visual material complements written tests.
- Repeat information or lessons loudly with eyes closed.
- Listening to music can help in studies.

- Record study material and listen to it frequently.
- Get involved in group discussions.

Kinesthetic Learners

Qualities of a kinesthetic learner

- Kinesthetic learners learn best by doing.
- They enjoy reading while performing another activity.
- Conversely, they enjoy physical action while reading or studying.
- Respond well on involving them.
- They are mostly good at sports.
- They notice body movements during discussions/meetings.
- They enjoy dancing while listening to songs or movies.
- They enjoy mechanical work.
- They can't sit still without doing something for too long.

They can do better in:

- Doing the task at hand
- Solving multiple challenges
- Activities involving movement
- Performing or creating activities

The issues faced by such learners are:

- Day-long discussions
- Writing or creating notes
- Remaining quiet for a long duration

Activity

Learn to juggle. Read the benefits of juggling above.

- To explore your creative skills, blindfold yourself and move around your house. Then note down what you have touched or felt without opening the blindfold:

  _____
  _____
  _____

- Involve yourself with other departments and learn new skills.
- Help others when you have free time.
- Study designs and check if you can add/modify something and add value to the product.
- Create flash cards about the process and see if you can learn to follow them.

Important tips

- Use practical approaches for learning.
- Learn effectively through different activities.
- Short sessions are more effective than longer ones.
- Use flash cards.
- Listening to music can reduce stress.

ANALYSIS: DATE: _____

Some people find that their learning style may be a blend of two or three styles. Fill the table below to help yourself understand your preferences and which learning style suits you well.

Reading: While reading, do you imagine what you read, or do you prefer reading loudly? Or do you like to act it out physically to understand better?

Writing: While writing, do you imagine (daydream), do you read while writing, or do you just go on writing?

Listening: While listening to any conversation, do you get engrossed and visualize, listen with your eyes closed, or try to figure out what has just been said?

Understanding: Do you understand concepts when they are picturized, do you understand them just by reading and repeating them, or do you understand them better by writing them down?

Using the VAK (Visual, Auditory, Kinesthetic) activities, observation and analysis, you can classify yourself and understand which learning style you prefer while performing the reading, writing, listening and understanding activities. The value should be rated on 10. (0 = Low, 10 = High)

Style	Reading	Writing	Listening	Understanding
V				
A				
K				

After two months, analyze yourself again based on the above parameters.

Summary

In this chapter, we have learnt:

- Assessment of our learning style
- Types of learning styles and working mechanisms
- The qualities and drawbacks of each learning style
- Activities for better performance

Chapter 6

Handling Successful Meetings and Discussions

Introduction

A 'mind map' is a technique that can help in compressing information, turning it into visual images and making it easy to process and remember. A mind map is a diagrammatic representation used to depict words, ideas and tasks around a central keyword or idea.

Creative mind mapping involves creating a graphical representation of images, shapes, colours, symbols, routes, etc. It's a simple method, where visual representation helps one distinguish words or ideas. It generally takes a hierarchical or tree-like format. Mind mapping allows greater creative and imaginative skills, as well as allowing the brain to associate words with visual representations. It is structured in a way that helps the brain to focus on individual road maps, routes or branches, thus facilitating proper understanding.

Most Common Style of Note-Taking

The most common style of note-taking uses just one colour, known as **MONOTONE.**

Monotone = Monotonous = NOT Brain-friendly.

A much better way to process our thoughts is to make a creative map!

Resources required for creative maps:

- Plain white paper—good quality A4 or A3 size
- Colour pens
- A colour pencil
- Highlighters

Practise

- Draw by moving the pencil
  - Only with your fingers
  - Only with your wrist
  - Only with your elbow
  - Only with your arms

Benefits

Mind maps are used to generate, visualize, structure and classify ideas. They are also used as aids in studying and organizing information, solving problems, making decisions and writing.

We can use mind maps for:

- Note-taking
- Brainstorming (individually or in groups)
- Problem-solving
- Planning
- Researching
- Presenting information
- Gaining insight on complex subjects
- Expressing our creativity
- Design layout
- Structure/relationship representations

- Collaboration
- Combination
- Team-building or synergy-creating activities
- Enhancing work culture and morale

Process

1. Start in the centre with an image of the topic, using at least two to three colours.
2. Use images, symbols, colours, codes and two or three dimensions throughout your mind map.
3. Use different cases for different key words—if possible, write them in different coloured pens.
4. Each word/image is best treated alone and within its own line.
5. The lines should be connected, starting from the central image. The central lines should be thicker and should grow thinner as they move out from the centre.
6. Make the lines the same length as the word/image they support.
7. Use multiple colours throughout the mind map, for visual stimulation and also to encode or group.
8. Develop your own personal style of mind mapping.
9. Show associations in your mind map.
10. Keep the mind map clear by using radial hierarchies, numerical orders or outlines around your branches.

An example of a mind map:

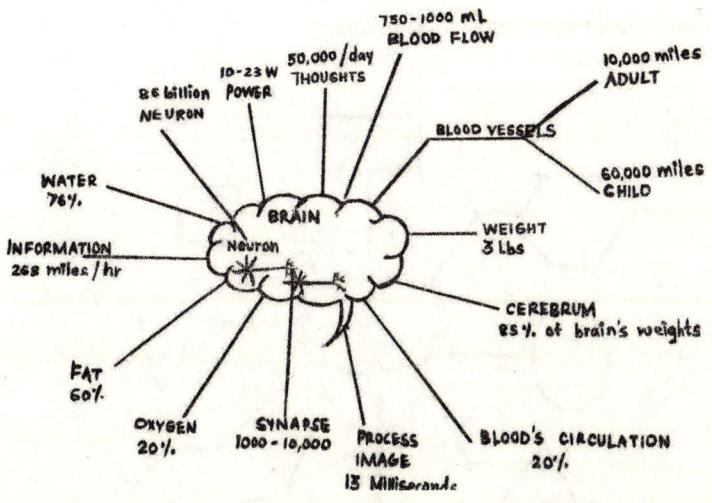

Activity 1

1. Take a plain sheet of paper. Start from the centre and create a mind map for yourself—your education, hobbies, likes, dislikes, experiences, etc.
2. You can even make a creative mind map of movies you have seen or heard about, according to their genre—romance, thriller, comedy, action, cartoon, horror, etc.

Use the following questions:

- What kind of movies do you like most?
- Why do you like them?
- What are your favourite movies?
- Why do you enjoy these movies?

Create your own mind map below.

Source: Pixabay

Activity 2

Aim: To create charts, memory images, blocks or creative representations of study material, content, etc.

Resource(s) required: A4- or A3-sized plain white sheet of paper, coloured pens, colours, highlighter

Process:

Take a magazine, and start reading and noting down the important words.

Summary

In this chapter, we have learnt:

- The most common style of note-taking
- Creative maps
- Practice exercises
- Benefits of mind maps
- The process of making mind maps
- Two mind mapping activities

Chapter 7

The Importance of Connections

Introduction

In our daily lives, we are connected to various groups and professionals and deal with lots of information every day. How can we effectively memorize and recall these myriad names, faces and connections?

Effective Mnemonics

Effective memorization systems are based on five main ingredients:

- Imagination
- Connectivity
- Association
- Senses
- Location

Imagination: Our mind can pursue anything. We create ideas through our imagination. Therefore, to sharpen our memory, we must create images that are simple, vivid and engaging. You could visualize a real incident or an event in order to remember and re use it, or invent one that will help you write, say or do something in the future.

Activity

Observe the images from your past memories and experiences and try to build images in your mind.

Alternatively, you can **make a list** of the important things in your life as you imagine them.

_____	_____
_____	_____
_____	_____
_____	_____
_____	_____
_____	_____

From the above list, make a drawing of significant icons, visuals or symbols in your life and combine them as an expressive self-portrait below:

Connection: Our memories are full of images, incidents, events and moments of loneliness or togetherness. Each of these is connected to something or the other.

For example, when we speak a single word, say 'Delhi', in a split-second all of our memories related to the word become active, as if we are in Delhi at the moment.

The places you visit, the people you meet, the restaurants where you have your breakfast/lunch/dinner, the hotels or houses where you stay, the transport systems you use for travelling from one location to another—these are the connections that our memories form.

Our memories get connected to each and every place we visit through the events that happen there and the people we meet.

Activity

Jot down a critical area of business you wish to improve and mark all the incidents, places, names, resources, etc. involved, as distinct points or dots. Connect the various dots and you will be surprised to see the picture emerging. Draw a pictorial presentation.

Critical area of business:

_____
_____
_____
_____
_____
_____

Connect the dots.

_____	_____
_____	_____
_____	_____
_____	_____
_____	_____

Association: Our brain is designed to link ideas, relations, activities, etc. Each unique piece of information can be linked, individually or in a group, to form a concept. By this process two ideas can be paired such that one thing reminds you of another.

For example: Thinking about growth in your business makes you also think of seasons, promotions, the people involved in relevant projects, etc. These associations further influence future decisions.

Activity 1

Write down the names of your clients and try to connect them with their profiles or companies.

Activity 2

Try to associate the names of your team members with objects that sound like their names.

For example: If one of your team members is called Mike, how can you recall his name?

Using the above strategy, imagine that he is on stage holding a microphone.

Note down similar examples from your life!

_____
_____
_____
_____
_____
_____

Senses: The senses play an important role in recalling images, sounds, voices and tastes, thus helping us remember the people we meet, the food we taste, etc. Each sense in itself has a direct connection to what we wish to recall.

Activity

Note down the important things you see, hear, feel, touch and taste. It shall help you during discussions, meetings and debates.

Location: Every location we visit is connected to certain memories and incidents. You can easily remember someone by connecting them to the location where you met them first, or vice versa. Locations thus help you not only remember both familiar and unfamiliar people, but also recall old memories as if they were happening at the moment. Since you can easily remember the layout of your home, why not associate each room in your house with an item, event or name from a list you are trying to memorize?

Activity

Note down the locations where your workplace conducts important presentations or meetings, and the objects at those locations, in a sequence. You can connect these objects and locations to points and slides in your presentations for enhanced recall.

For example: You have a conference at a hotel. As you enter the hotel, note down the location, objects and unique activities happening there in a sequence.

1. Reception   2. Big Clock   3. Staircase

Note them down below or draw pictures for future reference.

The Importance of Connections • 59

How to Remember Numbers through Connections

Many methods have been designed to help you understand and recall important points through connections. You can use any of these to recall points in presentations or meetings, topics to be discussed at conferences or seminars, your credit/debit card details, passwords, etc.

The CVSR method

C stands for CLICK—a word, object, scene or event that 'clicks' in your mind when you think of a particular number.

Think of what immediately clicks in your mind or brain when you think of the following numbers.

0—Could be a hula hoop or a bangle
1—Thumbs up, God, or father/mother
2—Bicycle (two wheels)
3—Rickshaw (three wheels)
4—..
5—..
6—..
7—..
8—..
9—..
10—...

V stands for VALUE—remembering any word, object, scene or event that has some value attached to it, and connecting it with a corresponding number.

1. One (or Ek in Hindi)—Eklavya, one-day matches, etc.
2. *Do Raaste*, twins, etc.

3. *3 Idiots*, Tiranga, etc.
4. ....
5. ....
6. ....
7. ....
8. ....
9. ....
10. ....

S stands for SHAPE—this is a method where you creatively mould a number into a shape that will help you recall the number or the associated shape easily at a later date.

1—Stick, pen, pencil, pole, etc.
2—Swan, coat hanger, etc.
3—Butterfly
4—..
5—..
6—..
7—..
8—..
9—..
10—...

R stands for RHYME—using words that rhyme with numbers to remember them.

One—Bun, gun, sun, etc.
Two—Shoe
Three—..
Four—..
Five—..
Six—..

Let us now look at a few systems to remember numbers through association, invented by prominent individuals in the field of memory.

The Musical Windows method, invented by Mr Vikrant Chaphekar

This is a phonetic method based on the musical notes Sa, Re, Ga, Ma, etc.

Musical Windows systems assign a number to the first letter of each of these notes (Sa, Re, Ga, Ma, Pa, Dha, Ni). So S-1, R-2, G-3, M-4, P-5, D-6, N-7, not repeating S since it has already been assigned 1. Now we need to assign alphabets to the numbers 8, 9 and 0.

We will use the logic that these seven notes of the Indian musical notation system are 'Taal' and the rest are 'BeTaal', so B-8, T-9 and L-0.

We shall not be using the letter 'X', since it has two syllables in itself (ak and sa), while all other alphabets have a single sound.

S	R	G	M	P	D	N	B	T	L
1	2	3	4	5	6	7	8	9	0

Now memorize and connect the alphabets to each number as assigned in the Musical Note Sequence.

Alternatively you can also use the Do, Re, Mi, Fa sequence and assign alphabets to numbers progressively to make it much simpler.

D	R	M	F	S	L	T	B	N	G
1	2	3	4	5	6	7	8	9	0

Assigning numbers in this manner can help connect any number with the alphabet.

Activity

Create 110 meaningful words, basically nouns (names, places, locations, imaginary things), from single digits (0 to 9) and then double digits (00 to 99).

For example:

No	MW	Word	Meaning	Description
1	S	Sea (one syllable)	Ocean	Deep large ocean
37	G,N	GuN	Weapon	Ajay Devgn holding a gun

The images thus created can be connected or associated with official activities such as presentation slides, minutes of a meeting, etc.

For example, if your fifth slide is related to your company's vision, we need to connect the word 'vision' to an image associated with 5 or the alphabet P. Here my chosen image is that of Pa—Amitabh Bachchan (AB) from the movie *Pa*. If you now imagine Pa or AB looking at something in the distance through his thick spectacles, you have successfully established a connection to 'vision'.

The Memory Filling system, invented by Dr Francis Xavier

This method of memorization was invented by Dr Francis Xavier, known as the 'Father of Memory'. I had the opportunity to work with him in various cities in a span of nearly two years. I feel honoured to have received a gold medal at the end of my training programme with him.

The Memory Filling system is completely based on relationships, emotions, and their connections.

The system basically associates numbers with the people you are close to, in descending order of closeness or importance.

For example,

1. Starts with God (or any other foremost relationship you share)
2. Mother
3. Father
4. Brother/Sister (elder)
5. Brother/Sister (younger)

And the list continues with paternal and maternal relatives, neighbours, friends, colleagues, etc.

You can even add film stars, sportspersons, etc. to the list.

The hierarchy or order of people, of course, depends on your personal relationships.

Once you have a list of a hundred people, you can then memorize slides, points, contact numbers, etc. accordingly.

Musical Walk

This system utilizes rooms and the people or objects in them to help you remember.

Let's assume that your connection points are other tenants or neighbours residing in the society/building/tower where you live.

1st Floor	2nd Floor	3rd Floor
101	201	301
Mr Singh	Mr Pawar	Mr Rodrigues
102	202	302
Mr Shah	Mr Barodawala	Mr Shaikh

Now in order to remember your slides during a presentation, you can connect/associate the relevant person with the slide title (determined by the number of the slide) and create an imaginary

64 • *Super Power Memory for the Busy Professional*

scene or story, to boost your recall during the presentation.

Mr Singh is welcoming all the guests in the society. This will help you to recall that the first slide is the welcome slide.

Mr Shah is a visionary person. He is practising shooting. This will help you to remember that the second slide is about the vision of the company, and so on.

Mai Hu Na method

This unique method is based on the parts of the human body, starting from the hair and going all the way down to the toes.

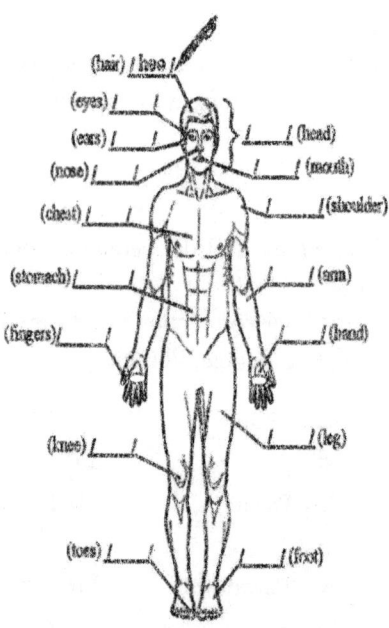

Suppose you wish to memorize your schedule for the day/to-do list. Here's how you can use this method.

1. 09:30: Call Mr Sharma
2. 09:45: Work on a financial proposal
3. 11:15: Meeting with Ms Rishita Khanna
4. 14:30: Presentation to committee members
5. 17:00: Leave for business meet at ITC Hotels

So here you can mix two or three methods together to memorize and recall the events in the sequence.

1. 09:30: Call Mr Sharma
   Let us associate the event with the topmost part of the human body—hair (as it is the first event in the itinerary).
   Now for the time (09:30)—
   By CSVR method, 09 can be associated with the shape of a balloon.
   By the Musial Windows method, 30 can be associated with the letters GL. Let us make the word 'goal' from those letters.
   Now you can create a bizarre story.
   Mr Sharma is balancing himself by the tip of his hair, as he is about to fall. Luckily, a balloon suddenly appears and lifts him high in the air. From there, he kicks a football, which zooms past the goalpost. There is a loud shout: 'GOAL!' This is followed by applause.

Similarly you can now create your own stories:

2. 09:45: Work on financial proposal.
   Event: Location:.............
   09: Shape: ....
   45: Musical Windows:......... : ....
   Story:
3. 11:15: Meeting with Ms Rishita Khanna
   Event: Location:.............

11: Shape: ....
   15: Musical Windows:.......... : ....
   Story:
4. 14:30: Presentation to committee members
   Event: Location:.............
   14: Shape: ....
   30: Musical Windows:.......... : ....
   Story:
5. 17:00: Start for business meet at ITC Hotels
   Event: Location:.............
   17: Shape: ....
   00: Musical Windows:.......... : ....
   Story:

Summary

In this chapter, we have learnt:

- Effective mnemonics
- Different methods of remembering numbers
- Various memory systems

Chapter 8

Understanding Intelligence

Introduction

Intelligence is hard to define. Almost all of us show intelligence in one way or another.

Do the questions below trouble you?

- Why is it that some people can do things better than others?
- Why can't we all be athletes?
- Why are some people more extroverted and comfortable with socializing than others?
- How can some people plan out their life so well?

Harvard University professor Howard Gardner's 'Theory of Multiple Intelligences' may answer all of these questions. According to his original theory, intelligence can be of multiple types, namely the following:[1]

- Linguistic
- Musical
- Logical
- Spatial

---

[1] https://www.personal.psu.edu/bxb11/MI/MultipleIntelligences_print.html

- Kinesthetic
- Intrapersonal
- Interpersonal
- Existential

Later, Professor Gardner proposed one more type of intelligence—naturalist—and a potential tenth, existential ('the intelligence of big questions').

The theory basically promotes the idea that every person has varying levels of aptitude in these nine categories. This is also partly cultural, as different cultures emphasize and promote different types of intelligence. In his book, *Frames of Mind*, Gardner provides the example of the high spatial abilities (i.e., a skill used for navigation, understanding or fixing any equipment, estimating distance and measurement, etc.) of a particular group of people in the Caroline Islands, who use these skills to navigate their canoes.

This theory, if correct, has radical implications for our entire education system, which mostly tests and trains people based on verbal-linguistic and logical-mathematical intelligence. Professor Gardner's theory can change our entire approach to education, pedagogy, and how we classify and teach students.

Multiple Types of Intelligence

How to Indentify Your Most Dominant Intelligence

Intelligence is hard to define, as it changes as per requirement. One can learn and unlearn anything according to one's need. Moreover, one can learn any type of intelligence through lessons and analysis and can acquire multiple intelligences at the same time.

Every individual is good at one thing or the other. We all

have the urge to do things, be it for personal satisfaction, to earn money, for pleasure or as a social activity. We need to identify our core skills and areas of interest—basically, what we are good at. This will help us determine our dominant intelligence and boost our ability to work and fulfil our life goals.

Let's say someone is good at speaking and explaining. If they work on communication skills, they can progress in the field of counseling. Similarly, others might be good at sports, creative activities, appreciating nature and wildlife, etc. One can identify the dominant intelligence of a person based on their individual preferences.

LINGUISTIC INTELLIGENCE

People with high verbal-linguistic intelligence are good at both speaking and listening. Consequently, they are good at storytelling and making their point. They have good memories for names, dates and places, and are skilled at wordplay, word games, reading and writing. They tend to become writers, speakers or teachers.

In the questionnaire below, tick the activities that you enjoy doing and give yourself 2 marks for each tick. Then fill in the table provided at the end of the chapter to know your dominant intelligence. This shall give you a fair idea of your intelligence. We have also provided you with some activities to improve your intelligence.

- Enjoy reading
- Love writing poems, plays, lessons, songs, etc.
- Like to talk, tell stories
- Remember names, dates and places
- Like to participate in debates and group discussions
- Enjoy learning new words and do so easily

- Be sensitive to the sounds of words
- Use various languages
- Excel in word game puzzles
- Like to explain the proper usage of words

Improve Your Skills

Activities

- Pay attention to the verbal styles of people you meet today in office and note down your views.
- Write down how you spend your day.
- Open a dictionary. Note down unfamiliar words.
- Note down words you use in your conversations everyday.
- Play word games (Scrabble, crosswords, anagrams).
- Attend a workshop on writing skills.
- Record yourself and listen to the playback.
- Go regularly to the library or bookstores.
- Maintain a diary and start writing on any subject.
- Attend a speed reading seminar.

MUSICAL INTELLIGENCE

Being musically inclined, people with musical intelligence are sensitive to the textures and patterns of the sounds in their environment, including those of the human voice. They learn and perform better when the lessons and tasks are accompanied by or delivered through music—like listening to music when studying/working. The most common examples of people with high musical-rhythmic intelligence are, unsurprisingly, singers, composers and musicians; but anyone showing a good grasp of music and rhythm can be said to have high musical intelligence.

In the questionnaire below, tick the activities that you enjoy doing, following the pattern given in the previous section.

- ☐ Like to listen to music
- ☐ Have a flair for music
- ☐ Play any musical instrument
- ☐ Interested in the sounds of nature, i.e., sounds of animals, trees, etc
- ☐ Can read when music is playing
- ☐ Able to perceive pitch and tone
- ☐ Have a well-developed auditory sense
- ☐ Can remember songs easily
- ☐ Able to sing or play instruments
- ☐ Have a knack for tapping and humming

Improve Your Skills

Activities

- Play 'name that tune' or other musical games.
- Use rhymes and songs to express your feelings.
- Put on background music while working.
- Make a list of all the music you hear in the course of the day.
- Go to a concert or a musical.
- Build a collection of your favourite musical records and listen to them regularly.
- Take a formal music lesson and learn a specific instrument. Work with a music therapist if you want.
- Spend a few hours a week listening to unfamiliar music (jazz, country, western, classical, folk, etc.)

LOGICAL INTELLIGENCE

People with high logical-mathematical intelligence tend to look for and explore patterns, links and rational connections. They are naturally inquisitive and orderly when it comes to work, and have high aptitude in working with numbers. They love solving problems through logical reasoning, and learn best through pattern recognition, orderly classifications and abstract thinking. As a result, people with high logical intelligence have come to be associated with what is commonly known as 'scientific thought', and tend to become scientists or mathematicians.

In the questionnaire below, tick the activities that you enjoy doing.

- ☐ Like mental calculations
- ☐ Like to solve mathematical problems
- ☐ Like to explore patterns, designs, puzzles, etc
- ☐ Find numbers and numerical symbols easy to use
- ☐ Think repeatedly and deeply before reaching a conclusion
- ☐ Like to reason before doing things
- ☐ Ask 'why' and 'how' questions
- ☐ Like to analyse before taking a decision
- ☐ Enjoy games with rules and regulations

Improve Your Skills

Activities

- Play logical-mathematical games with friends.
- Solve brainteasers and puzzles.
- Keep a calculator handy for figuring out math problems.
- Practice calculating simple math problems in your head.

- Read the business section of your daily newspaper.
- Read about famous math and science discoveries.
- Visit a science museum, a planetarium or other science centres.
- Engage yourself in blogs and groups that discuss scientific discoveries.
- Use blocks, beans or other concrete materials in learning mathematical concepts.
- Engage yourself in problem-solving and abstract thinking.
- Learn to solve complex visual and spatial problems.

VISUAL INTELLIGENCE

As the name suggests, people with high visual/spatial intelligence have a good grasp of spaces, work well with images, and have a knack for thinking visually. They are good at reading maps and charts and excel at the visual arts. They tend to be imaginative and creative, are good at designing things, and learn best through visual media like pictures and videos. Naturally, artists, architects, engineers, and other professions that require visual thinking (such as surgery) tend to have a higher concentration of people with high visual intelligence.

In the questionnaire below, tick the activities that you enjoy doing.

- ☐ Visualize images while thinking
- ☐ Visualize discussions even as you participate in them
- ☐ Love watching images, videos, pictures, etc
- ☐ Like drawing, painting, sculpting, etc
- ☐ Form images when trying to remember something
- ☐ Can orient yourself with maps or landmarks
- ☐ Use mind maps
- ☐ Enjoy designing and decorating

- ☐ Organize spaces, objects and areas
- ☐ Can translate the physical world easily into a new form

Improve Your Skills

Activities

- Use your phone camera to record your visual impressions.
- Create video presentations with a camcorder.
- Practise abstract thinking.
- Look for prominent images that you might not have observed before.
- Study maps and floor plans.
- Write down your ideas for being more productive at work.
- Develop your own visual symbols. Work with jigsaw puzzles, mazes or other visual puzzles.
- Learn photography.
- Pay attention to lights, camera movements, colours and other cinematic elements while watching movies and television shows.
- Take a class to learn drawing, painting, photography, video graphics, animation, 3D modelling, etc.
- Create 3D models of your ideas.
- Learn how to use flowcharts, tree diagrams and other forms of visual representation.
- Visit/work with architects, artists, and designers to see how they use their spatial abilities at work.
- Put your ideas and thoughts into pictures, graphics or visuals.

KINESTHETIC INTELLIGENCE

People who rely on their bodies to gather information, through physical senses and sensations, tend to have high kinesthetic intelligence. Naturally, they are good at physical activities and have a well-developed sense of balance and coordination. They learn best through hands-on lessons. People engaged in highly physical professions, such as mechanics, athletes, dancers, etc. tend to have high kinesthetic intelligence.

In the questionnaire below, tick the activities that you enjoy doing.

- ☐ Consider being an athlete
- ☐ Feel really good about being physically fit
- ☐ Exercise every day
- ☐ Play outdoor sports such as cricket, football or any other game
- ☐ Perform various activities such as aerobics, dancing, etc
- ☐ Experience strong mind-body coordination
- ☐ Experience total physical response
- ☐ Have awareness about movements of the body
- ☐ Can express emotions through body language
- ☐ Ability to handle objects with ease

Improve Your Skills

Activities

- Perform paper-folding activities.
- Practise yoga or other forms of relaxation
- Develop hand-eye coordination
- Take lessons in solo sports such as swimming, tennis, golf, etc
- Participate in sports-related activities
- Learn a martial art like judo or karate
- Exercise regularly. Play video games that require use of quick reflexes
- Take formal lessons in dancing

- Play charades with friends.

INTRAPERSONAL INTELLIGENCE

People with high intrapersonal intelligence are free thinkers with a strong sense of independence, and tend to be self-confident and keenly aware of their own flaws and strengths. They tend to have strong and firm opinions, and learn best by themselves rather than in groups, completing tasks or working at their own pace. High intrapersonal intelligence thus benefits entrepreneurs, philosophers and psychologists.

In the questionnaire below, tick the activities that you enjoy doing.

- ☐ Often look for weaknesses
- ☐ Like to be alone most of the time
- ☐ Like to note down ideas and work on them patiently
- ☐ Are self-motivated
- ☐ Find it difficult to get along with other people
- ☐ Are often a daydreamer
- ☐ Are good at self-planning
- ☐ Are good at setting goals
- ☐ Like to think alone, in quiet places
- ☐ Enjoy and appreciate self-discovery in isolation

Improve Your Skills

Activities

- Listen to a motivational speech or a podcast.
- Read self-help books.
- Write your autobiography.
- Always check your state of mind in a mirror.

- Practise meditation and yoga.
- Learn a new skill, language, etc.
- Find a quiet place in your home for introspection.
- Develop a hobby that sets you apart from the crowd.
- Set short- and long-term goals for yourself.
- If you are religious, regularly visit a house of worship of your choice.
- Do something enjoyable for yourself at least once a day.
- Spend time with people who have strong self-esteem.

Interpersonal Intelligence

People with high interpersonal intelligence are highly social, thriving in personal interactions and feeling most comfortable around other people. They tend to be popular and are able to conjure genuine empathy for others. Consequently, they have a knack for social activities and learn or work best in groups and through communication. Those with high interpersonal intelligence tend to make the best teachers, salespeople, leaders and organizers.

In the questionnaire below, tick the activities that you enjoy doing.

- ☐ Often look for positive aspects in yourself
- ☐ Like to be in a group rather than alone
- ☐ Like to share ideas and thoughts with others
- ☐ Like to communicate with people often
- ☐ Love to talk, counsel and give advice to others
- ☐ Easily make friends and enjoy the company of others
- ☐ Are able to get the perspective of another person
- ☐ Love to talk to and influence people
- ☐ Are able to handle conflicts
- ☐ Respond well to verbal as well as non-verbal communication

Improve Your Skills

Activities

- Meet one new person every day and interact with them.
- Discuss relevant topics.
- Look at different things from different perspectives.
- Maintain a contact list and stay in touch with the people on the list.
- Take a leadership role in your group.
- Organize group brainstorming sessions.
- Volunteer for activities of interest or join an NGO.
- Collaborate with one or more persons on a project of mutual interest.
- Have regular discussions with family and friends.
- Communicate with people on social networking sites.
- Strike up conversations with people in public places.
- Attend family, school or work-related reunion programmes or events.
- Observe how people interact at public places for fifteen to twenty minutes everyday.

NATURALISTIC INTELLIGENCE

True to the name, people with high naturalistic intelligence tend to be particularly sensitive to nature and work best outdoors, amidst natural surroundings. They are thus good at pattern recognition and categorization, like people with high logical intelligence, but also planners and organizers and have a good sense of their surroundings, combining traits associated with interpersonal and visual intelligence, but in their own unique way. They feel a deep sense of attachment to plants, animals, and nature in general,

Understanding Intelligence • 79

and learn best when working with these, in natural settings. Unsurprisingly, they tend to become biologists, geologists, paleontologists, environmentalists or even astronomers.

In the questionnaire below, tick the activities that you enjoy doing.

- ☐ Love plants and animals
- ☐ Like to be with nature
- ☐ Like the sound of birds and the wind
- ☐ Like to study birds, flowers, seeds, etc
- ☐ Are fascinated by insects and small animals
- ☐ Collect natural objects such as bugs, rocks, seashells, sticks, etc.
- ☐ Tend to have respect for all living beings
- ☐ Are a keen observer of the environment
- ☐ Have good sensory skills—sight, sound, smell, taste and touch
- ☐ Like having different pets

IMPROVE YOUR SKILLS

Activities

- Get to know the natural objects in your own house.
- Share what you know about nature.
- Observe the sounds of nature carefully.
- Prepare a list of animals, plants and birds in your area.
- Visit websites that provide info about nature (use keywords such as nature, birds, botany, etc.).
- Choose a specific type of plant, animal or bird and learn more about it from different sources.
- Investigate new aspects of gardening, landscaping, etc.

- Read nature magazines.
- Keep a journal to note down your observations.
- Visit and explore the natural world—forests, hills, beaches, etc.

Earlier, you had given yourself 2 marks for each tick on the activities that you enjoy doing. Now, fill in the table below to know your dominant intelligence.

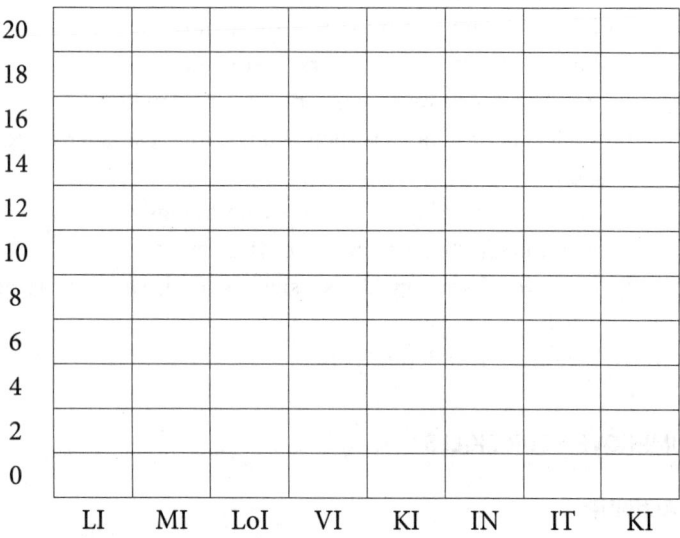

Summary

In this chapter, we have learnt:

- Types of intelligence
- Features of each type
- Activities to develop and hone each type

Chapter 9

Remembering Appointments

Introduction

Days and dates are integral to designing and scheduling our daily activities and commitments, planning events, celebrating occasions, completing particular tasks, etc. Learning the art of calculating the day for any given date helps an individual to respond easily, efficiently and quickly to any situation. This can make one sharper and more productive.

Let's learn a few techniques to mentally schedule our entire day on a particulate date.

DD-1 TECHNIQUE

This technique can be learnt easily by using logical thinking and a creative imagination.

Now let's explore:

Let us memorize the 2020 calendar by way of learning this technique.

Step 1:

Take a piece of plain paper and write down the months, one below the other, starting with January.

Step 2:

Take a calendar and write down the first day of each month in 2020, in the table below.

Sr. No.	Month	First day of the month
1	January	
2	February	
3	March	
4	April	
5	May	
6	June	
7	July	
8	August	
9	September	
10	October	
11	November	
12	December	

Tip: Observe that the first, eighth, fifteenth, twenty-second and twenty-ninth days of each month are the same day.

Step 3:

Now the question is, how do we remember that the first day of January 2020 is a Wednesday?

MEMORIZE IN A SEQUENCE

Now, let's make two more columns and note down a single unique or important event for each month—say, a national holiday, a birthday or an anniversary, a school or college event, etc.—and why the event is important. This can vary from person to person, depending on what day they consider important.

Month (2020)	First day of the month	Event	Association
January	Wednesday	National event	Republic Day
February			
March			
April			
May			
June			
July			
August			
September			
October			
November			
December			

Step 4:

Take the first letter of each day of the week.

SUN	MON	TUE	WED	THUR	FRI	SAT
S	M	T	W	T	F	S

Step 5:

Since Sunday and Saturday share the same first letter (S), as do Tuesday and Thursday (T), let us add the second letters for these days.

SUN	MON	TUE	WED	THUR	FRI	SAT
SU	M	**TU**	W	**TH**	F	**SA**

Step 6:

Now let us transform these letters into meaningful words, in order to form associations.

Observe:

SUN	MON	TUE	WED	THUR	FRI	SAT
Sunny	**Mon**ey	**Tue**	**Wed**ding	**Thur**st	**Fri**edom	**Sa**nd

Step 7:

Now let's connect the unique event we have chosen for each month with each word that corresponds to the first day of that month, by making up a story.

For example:

Month (2020)	First day of the month	Corresponding word	Event	Association
January	Wednesday	Wedding	Republic Day	On Republic Day, my parents/relative/friend got married.

By remembering the association we have made above between 'Republic Day' and 'wedding', we can now recall that the first day of January 2020 is a Wednesday.

Now, as long as we keep in mind that the first, eighth, fifteenth, twenty-second and twenty-ninth days of each month are the same, it becomes easy to calculate any other day and date simply by adding to or subtracting from those fixed dates. For example, if you need to calculate what day 19 January 2020 is, use the above association to recall that the first day of the month is Wednesday. Therefore, 15 January is also a Wednesday, and calculating up from that date, 19 January, which is four days later, will be a Sunday.

Imagine how you will feel when you can easily recall or calculate any day of any month using these steps!

Identifying the Day

What is the day on 19 January 2020?

Step A: January—Event: Republic Day
Step B: The event is associated with 'wedding', so the first day of the month is a Wednesday.
Step C: 1, 8, 15, 22 and 29 are all Wednesdays.
Step D: We need to calculate the day for 19 January 2020.

We can arrive at the date by doing either 15 + 4 or 22 - 3. Either way, we will arrive at Sunday.

So, 19 January 2020 is a Sunday.

Activity

Let us now calculate some random dates to see if you have learnt the process successfully. Check your answers on a calendar.

No	Date	Day
1	3 February 2020	
2	18 March 2020	
3	28 September 2020	
4	21 November 2020	
5		

Now it is equally important to remember the dates and times of meetings. You can do so by using any of these methods, described in Chapter 7:

- Musical Windows by Mr Vikrant Chaphekar
- Memory Filling system by Dr Francis Xavier
- Dominic system/Alphabet method
- Roman Room system/Musical walk
- Mai Hu Na method

Activity

Let's schedule a list of appointments/meetings/seminars/events and check if we can recall the day:

Date	Time	Event	Person of Interest	Location
1 January 2020	10:30	Meeting	Founder and CEO: Mr Alan Johnson	The Leela

Step 1:

Find out the day and determine a link word for it. In this case, the day is Wednesday and the link word is 'wedding'.

Step 2:

Create your unique story. For the time (10:30 a.m.), you can use the shape of the number 10 (a bat and a ball) and the word I linked to the number 30 using the Musical Windows method: 'goal'. Associate these with the person and the place.

Step 3:

Mr Alan Johnson has invited you for his wedding ceremony at The Leela. The couple shall be declared married on scoring a goal with a bat and a ball.

Now try out some of your own!

Date	Time	Event	Person's Name	Location

Summary

In this chapter, we have learnt:

- The DD-1 technique
- Association
- Identifying a date

Chapter 10

Faster Reading Speed

Introduction

If you can learn to just recognize words visually without having to repeat them mentally first, you can read much faster. As a professional, you might need to read a lot of news articles, statistical data, case studies, marketing information, analysis, resumes, etc. Expert speed readers can do all of this a bit faster than untrained people.

Take this short test:

• Do you skip words or lines while reading?	Yes	No
• Do you reread lines?	Yes	No
• Do you lose the place where you last stopped reading?	Yes	No
• Are you easily distracted while reading?	Yes	No
• Do you need to take breaks often?	Yes	No
• Do you find it harder to read the longer you read?	Yes	No
• Do you get headaches when you read?	Yes	No
• Do your eyes get red and watery?	Yes	No
• Does reading make you tired?	Yes	No
• Do you blink or squint?	Yes	No

- Do you prefer to read in dim light?   Yes   No
- Do you read close to the page?   Yes   No
- Do you use your finger or other markers?   Yes   No
- Do you get restless, active or fidgety while reading?   Yes   No

If most of your answers are 'YES', you have not mastered the art of reading.

Reading is a dynamic process between the page, the eye and the brain. It is a Brain-Mind-Eye Process that involves:

- Eye movement
- Character recognition
- Assimilation and understanding
- Remembering and recall

Reading is 20 per cent eye movement and 80 per cent thinking.

Here's how we can change some common reading practices for speed reading:

- Hopping: Movement of your eyes from one word to another. When you hop you are able to identify key words, which help in reading faster and better.
- Pausing: Normally while reading, we pause between two words to connect and associate them. In speed reading, we pause between two to three words to move faster while retaining proper understanding, instead of a single word at a time.
- Lingering: Readers usually linger when they have doubts, are unable to understand, or are not able to retain what they are reading. This is a slow process that lowers reading speed.

- Wondering: Letting your brain wander also reduces the speed of reading and understanding.
- Back-skipping: While reading slowly, there are involuntary back-skipping movements of the eyes and repeated readings of the same text, which reduce the speed of reading.

Reading Style (Untrained)

Aim: To understand one's reading style and speed.
Learning objective: To determine how an untrained reader reads and whether the reading style and speed are appropriate and match universal standards.
What you need: Magazine/Book, pencil.

What to do:

1. Take a magazine/book.
2. Set a timer for two minutes.
3. Now start reading a passage and stop after two minutes.
4. Count the number of words read.
5. Now divide that number by two, so that you get an average speed of words per minute (wpm).

Average speed per minute =
Date: _____ Time: _____

Find the speed reading score sheet below. Take at least five readings daily and note down the time required and how much you were able to comprehend.

SPEED READING SCORE SHEET

CHECK		I	II	III	IV	V
DATE						
COMPREHENSION	100 per cent					
	75 per cent					
	50 per cent					
	25 per cent					

READING SPEED: If you follow the correct reading techniques, you will most definitely improve your reading speed. If your reading speed for the first reading was, say, 230 WPM (words per minute), write this number next to 200 marks in the first (I) column, and your corresponding level of comprehension in the suitable box. The next time you test yourself, move on to the second column, and so on.

Now tick the appropriate boxes in the table below as per your reading speed per day, and you will have a progress chart showing your improvement.

READING	WPM	Day 1	Day 2	Day 3	Day 4	Day 5
	2000					
	1900					
	1800					
	1700					
	1600					
	1500					
	1400					
	1300					
	1200					
	1100					
	1000					
	900					

	800					
	700					
	600					
	500					
	400					
	300					
	200					
	100					

NOTE:

Learn the reading skill technique and practice the exercises and then repeat. It will enable you to improve your reading skills.

Characteristics of a Skilled Reader

1. Reads for specific purposes
2. They are critical of the matter they read
3. They are selective. The reader does not read word for word. They read for ideas and build thought sequences. Not all ideas or bits of information have equal importance; not all of the text is important. A skilled reader even skips parts or selects only the most important ideas that apply to their specific purpose.
4. Has a flexible approach to the matter: A poor reader has only one reading rate—the same slow rate. The important thing is to adapt our reading speed to our specific purpose. A skilled reader can remember the main points in preparation for a test—but reads fairly slowly after writing down the main points. However, social studies and English texts can be read much faster than science and mathematics. A skilled reader knows when to read fast and when slow.

5. Economizes on time: A skilled reader uses no more time than is necessary for them to accomplish their purpose in reading.

Speed Reading Statistics

An average student's speed is about 250 words per minute (wpm). But when a person is trained to read faster, they can comprehend much more than that. Speed helps you focus your attention on your reading, and you are able to grasp the topic much faster when it is practised properly—just as a person driving a car at a speed of 10 km/hr has more trouble concentrating than someone driving at 70 km/hr, since much of the speed is automated due to rigorous practice and regular driving. Speed automatically brings about a certain rhythm in your reading. Rhythm helps comprehension, and higher speeds force you to read by phrases rather than word for word.

- On an average, we read 200-240 wpm, with < 50-70 per cent comprehension.
- The benchmark is 400 wpm with comprehension of more than 70-80 per cent.
- Readers who can read 800-1000 wpm with more than 80 per cent comprehension are among the top 10 per cent of readers.
- Readers who read more than 1000 wpm are in the top 0.01 per cent.

By reading vertically down the page instead of using the age-old horizontal line-by-line movement, the audio-vocal reflexes are bypassed, the brain learns to interpret large blocks of information at a time, and psychological functions are put to their maximum use.

What is the Ideal Speed of Reading?

There is no ideal speed. Our reading speed should be flexible depending on the purpose and the complexity of the matter.

What controls your reading rate?

The eyes track wide across the page in all directions, and the mind takes in what the eyes see. The improvement of speed largely depends on how you utilize your eyes' movement. Use your eye movements effectively with a clear focus on what is expected from the content when you are reading. When you start reading, your eyes move from left to right—forward sweep, and later also move quickly from right to left—return sweep.

You will notice that your eyes move with jerky stop-go-stop-go movements while reading. You get the meaning of words only when your eyes pause, and not when they are moving. Our eyes, mind and brain see most clearly what they fixate on. The number of words you see at one glance is called your recognition span. The fewer times your eye pauses, the wider your recognition span. To improve your reading rate, you must decrease your fixation pauses by increasing your recognition span.

Poor readers read word for word. Average readers read a group of words, while speed readers develop a habit of forming a wider perspective.

Rules for Reading by Phrases

(a) Read in chunks—multiple words within the flow or span of a single thought.
(b) Read between the lines.
(c) Read rhythmically—train your eyes to move at a regular pace

or rhythm, from phrase to phrase, smoothly.
(d) Avoid too many breaks—it makes the reading slow and uncomfortable.

What are the Factors that Hinder Reading Speed?

(a) Talking to yourself – Reading words aloud or pronouncing them softly with your lips or other speech muscles definitely slows down your reading. Stop subvocalizing so you can read faster.
(b) Head movements – Keep your head still. Let the eyes move along the line in a series of fixations.
(c) Compulsive regression – Reading each word is like taking a step forward; to regress means to go back and forth every few steps. If a reader does not read with a specific purpose in mind, their eyes wander back and forth aimlessly, just as their mind does. Compulsive regression should not be confused with purposeful regression—when you reread a word or phrase in order to question or recall.
(d) If a reader has defective or weak eyesight, their eyes will blink constantly or start watering, and they may even have inflamed eyelids or headaches, after reading for quite a short while. Sometimes you may even find the text to be blurry and the print to be dancing. Make sure your eyes are in good health.

Reading at Leisure

Reading is necessary for your mental development as well as for your growth as a person. The mind needs to be continually fertilized and enriched with foreign matter, much like barren soil. We read for ideas, understanding and learning. Leisure reading widens your horizon, sharpens your perception, and increases your word power and knowledge. We must make reading a habit.

Let's make a simple analogy: If you read for at least fifteen minutes a day, then you invest 15*30 = 450 minutes or seven-and-a-half hours into reading in a month. This is equivalent to attending a workshop/seminar/conference every month.

Some useful tips:

1. Read selectively.
2. Read with understanding.
3. Create your own notes (diagrammatic, using icons, symbols, etc.).
4. Be clear about your purpose.
5. Know about the author to understand their views.
6. Swipe your finger over the words, slowly increasing the speed. This will help your brain keep up with the words faster and faster.
7. Start reading from the bottom of the text in reverse order. This will create new patterns in your brain.
8. Focus on the centre of the paragraph and move your eyes sideways; your mind will do the rest.
9. Trust your brain. It is highly capable of putting words in the right order.

Reading Process

Reading is an art and we all need to learn it, same as other activities or games. Reading involves synchronization of the eyes, the mind and the brain.

Eye Movements

- Move your eyes, stop and re-read the text in order to comprehend better. This stopping or pausing of the eye movement is called 'fixation' or 'visual bite'.
- Every eye stop is known as 'fixation'. This pause is when the reading matter is recognized, understood, and stored in our memory.

Benefits of Eye Movements

- Concentrating in noisy settings
- Clear understanding of long and complex sentences
- Grasping difficult words
- Memorizing text and formulae
- Better recall
- Appreciating superb writing
- Helps to understand and remember important material

Information

Once your eyes learn how to move correctly, your brain will gobble up information on the page. This means:

- Reading faster = understanding faster
- Reading more = understanding more
- Read slowly and carefully
- An average person reads 200-240 WPM and understands 50-70 per cent

Tips

- Do not read word for word. Read in clusters or groups of words at a time.

- Keep moving forward.
- Keep your eyes and your mind on the page.
- No lingering at words, pictures or white space on the page.
- Minimize the pauses between groups of words.
- Use visual guides (charts of symbols) to speed up your eye movement.
- Read in good lighting.
- Keep your eyes 18-20 inches away from the reading material.
- Place the reading material on a surface sloping 20 degrees horizontally.
- Read in a well-ventilated space.

Now, for some strategies of reading:

1. **Determine your purpose.**
   Is you purpose to...
   - Review notes
   - Learn new stuff
   - Get facts
   - Seek opinions/advice
   - Entertainment
   - Confirm a belief
2. **Sit correctly.**

Your reading posture is extremely important. Your posture determines your

- Mood
- Speed of reading
- Comprehension
- Memory

Avoid slouching while reading. Don't stand, move, or sit in a lazy, drooping way.

Speed Reading Activities

Proper Reading

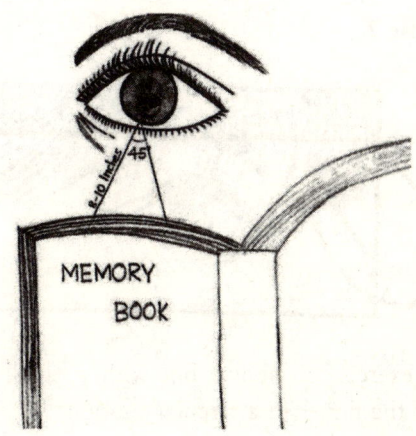

Hold a book in front of you at a 45 degree angle and about 8-10 inches away. Focus on the words.

Finger Exercise 1

Make a small dot on a finger and move it around. Your eyeballs should move in the direction of the dot. You can ask someone to do this for you, or you can do it yourself.

Finger Exercise 2

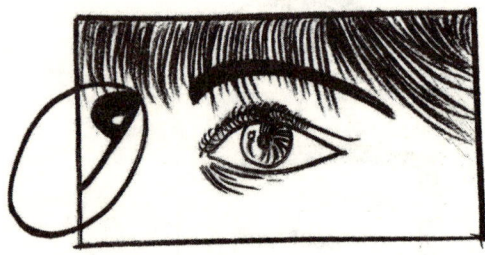

Same finger exercise as above, but with a small change—the movement of the finger in a circular motion.

Exercises to Improve Peripheral Vision

Memorize in Sequence

- Move your eyes between the pictures in this order: Car–Flower–Pen–Butterfly.
- Do it about ten times.
- Repeat the exercise but the change the pattern to: Car–Pen–Flower–Butterfly
- Repeat the exercises following other patterns.

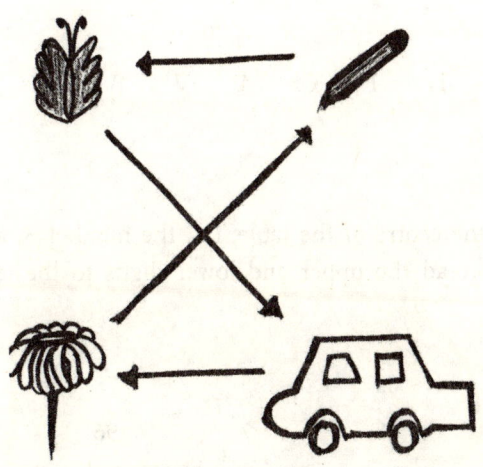

Daily Practice

Focus on the dot below, in the middle of the picture, and without moving your eyes, read out the letters around the dot aloud.

                Kor

Aba   Ima

Sir   ●   Ima

Sat   Ram

                Ron

Daily Practice

Focus on the centre, i.e., the letter A, and check if you can read the letters to the left and the right.

TEST A:

G   T   H   I   C   **A**   V   B   M   P   S

TEST B:

Focus on the centre of the table, i.e., the number 3, and check if you can read the upper and lower digits to the left, centre and right.

64	5	78
58	7	96
24	<u>3</u>	88
44	9	26
17	2	69

Activity

Now, read the following quickly:

The	two
Stop	method
Invented by	Wade E Cutler
and the main technique	is to minimize the eye
movement. Instead of reading by	each word separately, try
looking at every line twice only line,	First after the first third of the
and second after the third third.	That speed reading exercise will

a increase your reading speed and your eyes will not be exhausted. If you will keep practice this method, you will be able to read full lines without moving your eyes!

Believe me, it's possible!

Action Plan to Master Speed Reading

1. You can find printed material in abundance. This has resulted in the necessity to read with greater speed and understanding becoming sine qua non or an essential condition in the present day.
2. The aim of reading is to be able to read a word fluently and understand its meaning. Reading is an active, positive acquisition of ideas and this means the reader analyses, anticipates, compares, contrasts and evaluates.
3. The common impediments to speed and comprehension are: slow, laborious horizontal reading; the subconscious habit of mentally uttering each word; moving the vocal chords, throat muscles, and lips; regression, i.e., reading first and then looking back to determine what has been read and swinging the head from side to side.
4. By reading vertically down the page instead of using the age-old horizontal line-by-line movement, the brain learns to interpret large blocks of information at a time.
5. Our mind has the ability to derive the complete meaning of incomplete images or sentences.
   For example,
   CHENAI S TH CAPTL OF TAMNADU.
   Our mind is able to bridge the gaps with little or no loss of meaning.
6. The rate at which our mind can interpret the symbols seen by our eyes is not the same in all individuals.
7. Nothing is more limiting to success than anxiety and doubt. Only with a relaxed and receptive attitude can we reach the goal of speed reading.
8. To increase our comprehension, we should increase our concentration. To increase concentration, we should increase

our reading speed to be as close to our thinking speed as possible.

9. We can implement an entirely new approach to develop speed reading. Our eyes must now learn to take in an overall view while seeming to not concentrate on particular words and components. The mind becomes active in anticipating, demanding, assembling and comprehending large blocks of information while the eyes float smoothly down the page, stopping imperceptibly here and there as and when necessary to see larger and larger blocks of print.

10. Skipping and skimming are other methods of speed reading. They are not haphazard, helter-skelter methods of reading. They are well-defined skills and products of conscious and continued practice.

11. Skipping is getting the essence of the reading material without reading all of it. It involves judicious and selective skipping of non-essential matter. It is not careless—rather, it involves careful reading of selected words, sentences, etc. Knowing what to look for and how to pick it calls for an attitude, a technique and some judgement.

12. Skimming is gathering what we want as we 'fly' along, 'catching' what we desire, as if we are 'on wings'. Survey or preview is a primary step in the skimming process. We should also identify patterns of writing and find the main idea in a paragraph. We have to cultivate a willingness to skip large portions of content without, in any sense, feeling guilty.

13. Correspondences, memorandums, reports, newspapers, professional publications and books of different categories can be dealt with much more efficiently each day, if you acquire the skill of speed reading.

Activity

Weather Report

Read the following weather report and then answer the questions below:

Now comes our local weather report. Unlike other cities in the region, Sholapur continues to experience rain with temperature between 18 to 25 degrees. In Nasik, it is sunny in the morning, with thunderstorms in the late afternoon. The highest temperature will be 31 degrees and the lowest 24 degrees. Pune is slightly cooler today. It is cloudy with a temperature of 28 degrees in the day. Overnight, the temperature will drop down to 18 degrees.

Now answer following questions.

1. How is the weather in Sholapur region?

   _____
   _____
   _____

2. What is the lowest temperature in Pune?

   _____
   _____
   _____
   _____

3. What is the highest temperature in Nasik?

   _____
   _____
   _____
   _____

4. Where is thunderstorm in the late evening?

   _____
   _____
   _____
   _____

Summary

In this chapter, we have learnt:

- How to read better
- Following regular eye exercises to improve reading speed
- Better ways to improve reading speed

Chapter 11

Creative Thinking

Introduction

Creative thinking is the process of creating new activities from our experiences, knowledge and learnings, by applying innovative ideas.

Creativity can be defined as the ability to go beyond traditional ideas, rules, patterns, relationships or the like, and to create new ideas, forms, methods, interpretations, etc. Originality, progressiveness and imagination are three things that are needed for creativity in the modern world.[1]

Extensive reading can stimulate creativity.

Creative Test

This is a simple and fun test to see how creative you are—at the moment!

1. I understand the difference between logical thinking and creative thinking:
   ○ Never   ○ Occasionally   ○ Frequently   ○ Always

2. I use creative techniques to stimulate my thinking patterns:
   ○ Never   ○ Occasionally   ○ Frequently   ○ Always

---

[1] https://www.dictionary.com/browse/creativity

3. I challenge the accepted ways of doing things:
   ○ Never   ○ Occasionally   ○ Frequently   ○ Always

4. I come up with creative ideas on a daily basis:
   ○ Never   ○ Occasionally   ○ Frequently   ○ Always

5. I have a variety of creative thinking tools in my thinking toolkit:
   ○ Never   ○ Occasionally   ○ Frequently   ○ Always

6. I asked lots of questions when I was a child:
   ○ Never   ○ Occasionally   ○ Frequently   ○ Always

7. I still ask lots of questions:
   ○ Never   ○ Occasionally   ○ Frequently   ○ Always

8. I use mind maps:
   ○ Never   ○ Occasionally   ○ Frequently   ○ Always

9. I spend time daydreaming:
   ○ Never   ○ Occasionally   ○ Frequently   ○ Always

10. I have a good memory:
    ○ Never   ○ Occasionally   ○ Frequently   ○ Always

11. I have a naturally curious nature:
    ○ Never   ○ Occasionally   ○ Frequently   ○ Always

12. I mix with people outside my field:
    ○ Never   ○ Occasionally   ○ Frequently   ○ Always

13. I find it easy to visualize things in my mind's eye:
    ○ Never   ○ Occasionally   ○ Frequently   ○ Always

14. I try to define problems in several different ways:
    ○ Never   ○ Occasionally   ○ Frequently   ○ Always

15. I am aware of my preconceptions and know how to overcome them:

○ Never ○ Occasionally ○ Frequently ○ Always

16. I see difficult problems as a challenge, not an obstacle:
    ○ Never ○ Occasionally ○ Frequently ○ Always

17. I am able to think outside the box:
    ○ Never ○ Occasionally ○ Frequently ○ Always

18. I am willing to listen to someone else's ideas:
    ○ Never ○ Occasionally ○ Frequently ○ Always

19. I am good at searching my mind for new solutions to old problems:
    ○ Never ○ Occasionally ○ Frequently ○ Always

20. I take the time to think creatively before analysing ideas logically:
    ○ Never ○ Occasionally ○ Frequently ○ Always

21. I believe in the impossible if I want it badly enough:
    ○ Never ○ Occasionally ○ Frequently ○ Always

22. I take opportunities to do new things:
    ○ Never ○ Occasionally ○ Frequently ○ Always

23. I attempt thinking puzzles:
    ○ Never ○ Occasionally ○ Frequently ○ Always

24. I try to adopt a different way of doing something every week:
    ○ Never ○ Occasionally ○ Frequently ○ Always

25. I regularly visualize my goals and I find this helps me to solve problems:
    ○ Never ○ Occasionally ○ Frequently ○ Always

26. I keep looking for new ideas, even when I have found a potential solution:
    ○ Never ○ Occasionally ○ Frequently ○ Always

27. I believe that even good habits can be barriers to creativity:
    ○ Never   ○ Occasionally   ○ Frequently   ○ Always

28. I believe that people not involved in an issue can offer insights:
    ○ Never   ○ Occasionally   ○ Frequently   ○ Always

29. I think that it is necessary to take time out to be creative:
    ○ Never   ○ Occasionally   ○ Frequently   ○ Always

30. I read widely on unrelated topics:
    ○ Never   ○ Occasionally   ○ Frequently   ○ Always

31. I take pride in being creative and I encourage others to be creative:
    ○ Never   ○ Occasionally   ○ Frequently   ○ Always

32. I believe that it is possible for everyone to be creative:
    ○ Never   ○ Occasionally   ○ Frequently   ○ Always

Activity 1

Your subconscious mind is powerful. Visualize and create an imaginary picture of two unrelated concepts and create an association between them, leading to a unique, new idea. Put your creative subconscious mind to work.

Example: 'Hospitals' and 'swimming':
Patients are treated while they swim.

Your idea:

___

'Book' and 'carpenter':
Carpenters design creative books for professionals.

Your idea:

___

Activity 2

Think of ten random things and list them:

1. _____
2. _____
3. _____
4. _____
5. _____
6. _____
7. _____
8. _____
9. _____
10. _____

Combine the above things in any way you can think of.
First phase: Two at a time   Second phase: Three at a time

Creative Concepts

How to be creative:

Creative tools can help design a new product, spark business ideas or catalyze innovations. Most such ideas come from combinations and connections.

Finding new applications:

TV is used as a tool for entertainment. What other use of TV can we think of? Maybe as a virtual reality gaming device that replicates a space shuttle, where we can enter and enjoy a space ride.

The key is to find new ideas, new applications and new uses for existing ideas!

Finding cost-effectiveness:

Can the material/equipment used in the TV set be replaced with a cheaper material, say plastic or cardboard, without compromising on the quality of the picture?

Can it be more compact if it was stretched or compressed to save space?

This leads to several benefits:

- Saving of space
- Compatibility
- Portability
- Cost-effectiveness

Can we think of ideas that we once felt were impossible, but are realities today?

Example: In UK, there is an open prison.

Idea 1: ———————
Idea 2: ———————
Idea 3: ———————
Idea 4: ———————
Idea 5: ———————

Let's think of new ideas for regular objects.

a. Can you think of new uses for scrap paper?

———————————————————————
———————————————————————
———————————————————————

Creative Thinking • 113

b. Can you think of creative uses for electric wires?
    _____
    _____
    _____

Generating New Thoughts

We see things a certain way and never question their purpose or existence, since we have become accustomed to using those things only for those specific purposes.

Can we challenge the purpose or existence of a thing?

The simplest way is to look at things and ask: What if _____(it's bigger, smaller, cheaper, etc.)?

Take notes as you fill in the blank. Most words may not give you the desired output or results, but don't reject any idea. Creative solutions can begin with unrelated thoughts.

You can add hundreds of ideas to the list. Any adjective, verb, descriptive phrase or word that can change your perspective can be used.

Activity

What if: Books can
see _____
_____
walk _____
_____
feel _____
_____
cook _____

How Creatively Can You Think?

What if employees were allowed to work from home?

_____

_____

_____

Benefits

_____

_____

_____

Disadvantages

_____

_____

_____

What will change?

_____

_____

_____

You can add a few more questions based on your interactions with others.

Activity

Best from waste

Design a unique product that is compact, useful, user-friendly and unique, using the list of items below. Draw as many designs as possible.

1. Lamp
2. Laptop

3. Dining table
4. Temple
5. Comfortable chair

Activity

Situation 1:

You encounter a tiger that has just escaped from the zoo. To your astonishment, it speaks to you! Imagine your conversation with the tiger. Use these questions to help you.

1. How do you feel when you first hear the tiger speaking?
2. What does the tiger try to say to you?
3. Do you decide to help the tiger?
4. What do you do?
5. What happens in the end?

_____
_____
_____
_____
_____

Situation 2:

Write about a day when you felt very happy. Use these questions to help you.

1. Do you remember the exact month and year?
2. Was it a special occasion or celebration?
3. What happened that day?
4. How did you react to the things that happened?

5. How did other people react when they saw you were so happy?
6. What did you do next?
7. What happened in the end?

___

Describe any other emotions you felt that day.

___

Summary

In this chapter, we have learnt:

- How to be creative
- How to ideate
- To generate new thoughts
- How creatively we can think

Chapter 12

Connecting and Engaging with Customers

Introduction

A person's distinctive features can be represented using their job or hobby.

For example, if you want to memorize information about a cleaner, he can be represented by a broom. A person playing classical music might be represented by a sitar, and so on.

When you choose a distinctive feature, you should try to think of a relevant image that distinguishes the person from others.

A connection between a face on a photo and the distinctive feature you select does not need to be consciously memorized, because when you examine a photo and the distinctive feature you selected, you perceive several images at the same time. You only need a couple of seconds to attentively examine the face and pay attention to the selected distinctive feature.

The distinctive features themselves are simple visual images that need to be memorized consecutively.

When you remember a sequence of distinctive features, you make your brain generate other images connected to that sequence—that is, faces. That is how simple this memorization technique is.

You can memorize a sequence of pictures analogically—even pictures at an exhibition.

Name stands for nominate, articulate, morph and entwine.

Nominate: Pick a photograph.

First of all, let's explore the challenge of closely looking at a person's face and identifying a key feature.

There are a couple of ways to deeply examine a face.

1. First look closely at that particular face and mentally draw the letter Z across it. Start at the eyes and eyebrows on the left, zip across to the right, diagonally across the nose, then left to right across the mouth.
2. Another is to mentally draw a figure eight, circling down from the eyes to the mouth and reverse again.

Practise this skill when looking at people when you are out, or on television or pictures in newspapers and magazines. As you practice this study of faces, you will develop your own facial vocabulary to describe a person's features.

Articulate: Speak and repeat, fluently and clearly.

Repetition is a key to success. When the other person introduces themselves, be aware and conscious when listening to the name. Repeat the name clearly, so that you understand it properly. Check for the sound and accent by repeating the alphabets again. Over the course of your conversation, repeat the name again and again.

For example:

Hello, Mr Robert. Nice connecting with you.

Where do you stay, Mr Robert?

How is the weather today, Mr Robert?

Morph: Change smoothly and gradually from one image to another.

How can you convert names (with no intrinsic meaning) into something memorable?

1. Switch a few letters around: For example, the name 'Harper' could be transformed into 'Helper' with the addition of an 'e' and an 'l' and thus Harper's morphed name could be Helper. Try adding a vowel or two (a, e, i, o or u) to the name. Another way to memorize is to break the word into two words, e.g., HAR + PER. We can morph HAR to 'Hari' and 'PER' to 'Perk' for better recall.
2. Rhyme: By building up your vocabulary, you can find appropriate rhymes for almost any name. For example, the name 'Hans' can be transformed to 'Fans'. Morphing names is going to depend on your personal history, background, education and the associations you have built in your life. Use wordplay to transform the name. Ask yourself, 'What does it sound like or remind me of?' A few great ways to build your vocabulary are solving crossword puzzles, reading the dictionary, etc. This also exercises your mind and keeps it awake to new ways of looking.

Making effective name morphs:

1. Begin with a letter of the name you are morphing.
2. Try to choose similar-sounding objects, rather than verbs or adjectives.
3. Choose different objects every time you visualize or imagine.
4. When necessary, you can make an effective morph by using an image inspired by the name.
5. Be imaginative: What does the name sound like? Use rhymes, images, etc. Think differently.
6. If the name seems overwhelming, break it down into one-syllable components.

Morphs enable you to see names that normally you only hear.

More interest in names leads to a better chance of remembering them.

Create your own list of morphed names and review it regularly. It is a good idea to have the same morph for the same name, as this is your personal collection of name images.

Entwine: Wind or twist together.

Connect the name and face of a person and create a unique image or symbol. This will help you recall more easily.

For example: To remember Mr Mark, visualize the marks on his face, hands or legs.

Tools to Remember Names and Faces:

1. **Focus on the name:** Sometimes simply using a name can help one remember it, rather than focusing on the tools of memory such as combinations or connections. Using a person's name creates a connection and turns it into something special and of value.
2. **Be aware:** You need to listen to the name of the person properly at the first instance. If it is not clear, ask for more clarity; spell it out loud. Pay attention and listen with full awareness to remember and recall later. The trick is to focus completely on the person to whom you are talking, and not on yourself. Most of the time, we are in such a hurry to jump to the topic that our focus shifts to something else. Be aware of one thing that you need to remember—the name of the person—and in that process, build your memory.
3. **Ask:** One very important thing to do is ask. Ask for their name and understand the pronunciation. Ask for the name again if you don't hear it correctly the first time. Seize the moment, be sure to say that you 'didn't catch the name', or

something similar, right away. Listen well the second time. It is a good practice to apologize and ask for a repeat if you are overwhelmed by nervousness, noise, disturbance or any other distraction.

4. **Repetition**: Repeat the person's name when you are introduced. Do this slowly to make it clear. During the conversation, try to use the name as many times as possible, either in the beginning of the sentence or in the end.

   For example:
   Mr Ramesh, can you tell us more about your company?
   or,
   We have heard about your products, Mr Ramesh.
   Repeating the name at least three times can help you register it in your memory.

5. **Connections**: Associate the name with a person you know—maybe a neighbour, a colleague or a friend. Create a mental picture connecting the new person to a familiar one, perhaps with a similar name (or even a celebrity or a sportsperson). When you need to recall the name, you can visualize this mental picture.

6. **Look for prominent features**: Study the person and try to notice any features or prominent aspects. Maybe the way he dresses is similar to a famous TV star, or maybe the way he speaks reminds you of a friend. Making such connections will help you recall their name in subsequent meetings.

7. **Study the distinctive features on the face**: By observing the face you can visualize some prominent marks or the structure of the face. Examine the hair, the colour of the skin or any other characteristic while talking. Try to find something easy to remember about them, such as jagged teeth, eyebrows, deep wrinkles, or anything else that is unusual or distinctive.

Try to associate the name with this feature, so that you remember next time.

For example, Mr Sharma has a broad smile that reveals all his teeth.

8. **Take your partner's help**: If you are not able to determine a unique feature, discuss with your partner or friend and take their help. Explain to them the importance of remembering the name of the person and try to figure it out with the help of their advice and suggestions.

9. **Trust yourself**: It's very important to trust yourself after you have registered the name. Your neurons transmit the information and store it for future use. Trusting yourself strengthens the connections and motivates the brain to perform at the right time.

Benefits of Remembering Names and Faces

1. The other person appreciates you.
2. Most people like it if they are addressed by their names.
3. Remembering the right name at the right time can benefit you.
4. It can sharpen your memory.

Summary

In this chapter, we have learnt:

- That NAME stands for Nominate, Articulate, Morph and Entwine
- To make effective name morphs
- About tools to remember names and faces
- The benefits of remembering names

Chapter 13

Positive Stress

Introduction

What causes stress?

Stress is caused when we create or anticipate a situation that places on us the burden, pressure and fear of adverse consequences. Lack of confidence, money shortage, etc., are some reasons behind stress, and we call them stressors. Stressors are usually perceived to be negative, such as an exhausting work schedule, meetings, competition, taxing relationships, etc., as these things generally negatively affect our mental health and peace. But anything that places high demands on you can be stressful.

Can there be good stress?

Good Stress vs Bad Stress

The so-called 'good stress', or what psychologists refer to as 'eustress', is the type of stress we feel when we are excited. There are many triggers for good stress, and it keeps us feeling alive and excited about life.

Eustress means beneficial stress—either psychological, physical (e.g., with exercise), or biochemical/radiological (hormesis). The term, coined by endocrinologist Hans Selye, consists of the Greek prefix 'eu' meaning 'good', and stress, literally meaning 'good stress'.

An example of eustress would be a challenging but creative work assignment that is perceived, with a positive approach and mindset, to be neither too difficult nor too easy.

Another example would be a strength-training workout regimen that is enjoyable with regular productive breaks, rather than exhausting and tiresome.

Distress, on the other hand, is a negative form of stress—the one that we most commonly associate with stress.

When can stress be useful?

Positive stress can help you accomplish tasks more efficiently, since you wholeheartedly create new opportunities by opening your mind to capture ideas and thoughts. It can even boost memory. Stress is also a vital warning system, producing fight-or-flight response. When the brain perceives some kind of stress, it starts flooding the body with chemicals like epinephrine, norepinephrine and cortisol.

Here are a few tools to help manage the 'bad' stress:

1. Start your day with meditation and mindfulness yoga.
2. Take responsibility for improving your emotional, social and physical well-being.
3. Practise gratitude for the little and big things that happen throughout the day.
4. Relax at regular intervals to relieve pressure. Take an exercise break.
5. Socialize and move around during the day.
6. Get a good night's sleep.

Benefits of eustress:

We are quick to blame stress for a variety of problems, such as heart disease, ulcers, abdominal obesity and dementia. However, stress can be healthy, as Hans Selye mentions, and can give one a feeling of fulfilment, or other positive feelings.

How can I lift my mood?

1. Appreciate your small successes.
2. Flip through old memories.
3. Find ways to keep yourself happy.
4. Consciously inhale and exhale at least thrice a day.
5. Open your idea box.
6. Walk around with a smile on your face.
7. Clear away clutter.

Why do we need good stress?

When we are stressed, the heart beats faster, blood pressure increases, senses sharpen, a rise in blood glucose invigorates us and we are energized. It can improve heart function and make the body resistant to infection, according to experts. Far from being something we need to eliminate from our lives, good stress stimulates us.

The Four Common Types of Stress:

1. Time stress:

During project deadlines an employee/employer feels the burden of having to complete the work in the stipulated time frame.

Rushing for timely completion can reduce efficiency. Moreover, quality can be compromised or extra resources might have to be used, resulting in an increase in cost.

Let's analyse what can be done:

- Prepare a to-do list.
- Create a project time frame chart.
- Design a work flow with time slots.
- Manage the project timeline.
- Prioritize the task and complete it before the deadline.
- Maximize your productivity by working on important and complex tasks when you are most productive.

2. Anticipatory stress:

A lot of times, at a workplace, employees are worried and stressed about events that haven't occurred yet. FEAR (False Experiences Appearing Real) can stem from a present situation, uncertainty, personal drawbacks, etc.

Let's analyse what can be done:

- Make a contingency plan and prepare for worst-case scenarios.
- Work out positive solutions for future events.
- Upgrade yourself by registering for a programme/certificate course.

3. Situational stress:

This type of stress occurs when you are put in a critical situation without support, or you stop believing in your own abilities—maybe a situation where you feel handicapped because you are not being understood/listened to properly.

Let's analyse what can be done:

- Unlike other kinds of stress, this stress comes as a surprise, and hence preparation is less likely to help.
- It is important to have full control on your emotions, behaviour and tolerance.
- Communication can be used as a tool to express yourself and find a workable solution.

4. Encounter stress:

This stress can occur if you find it hard to deal with your subordinates, your boss or your customers, maybe due to personal dislikes, difference in opinions, seniority or other uncommon views.

Let's analyse what can be done:

- Developing strong interpersonal skills is the key to overcoming this type of stress.
- Intelligent moves or emotional intelligence can help you understand the other person better.

What is the Best Way to Cope with Stress?

Here are some healthy ways you can deal with stress:

1. Take care of yourself. Eat healthy, well-balanced meals.
2. Talk to others. Share your problems and how you are feeling and coping with a parent, friend, counsellor, doctor, etc.
3. Avoid drugs and alcohol.
4. Take a break.

Seven Ways to Get Happier in Less Than a Minute

1. Go for some chocolate!
2. Think of a loved one.
3. Recite a positive affirmation, such as, 'I will…,' or 'I'm going to…'
4. Do a quick forty-five second meditation.
5. Make a short gratitude list.
6. Have a thirty-second dance party.

How Can I Increase My Happy Hormones?

Here are the top four ways to naturally increase your happy hormones!

1. Reduce Stress: The biggest killer of your serotonin is stress.
2. 5-HTP: Serotonin is made from an amino acid called tryptophan, which is found in rich protein sources like meat, cheese and eggs.
3. Sunshine: Start your day by observing the sunshine, and let the rays fall on your body.
4. Massage: Best way to relax the body, mind and the brain.
5. Exercise: Regular exercises can help increase happy chemicals.

Summary

In this chapter, we have learnt:

- The causes of stress
- Good Stress vs Bad Stress
- A few tools to help manage bad stress

Positive Stress • 129

- Benefits of eustress
- How to lift your mood
- Why we need stress
- Four common types of stress
- Seven ways to get happier in less than a minute
- How to increase your happy hormones

Chapter 14

Meditation and Relaxation

Introduction

Meditation is a tool for mindfulness, or focusing your mind on a particular object, thought or activity. It relies on and builds the ability of the mind to enhance attention and awareness and achieve a mentally clear and emotionally calm and stable state. A state of mindfulness can be achieved through regular and consistent practice.

Relaxation is that emotional state of a living being in which there is an absence of arousal that could come from sources such as anger, anxiety or fear. According to the Oxford Dictionary, relaxation is when the body and mind are free from tension and anxiety.

There are different ways to achieve a relaxed mind and body—for example, taking a bath in hot water, listening to music, playing a musical instrument, sleeping, massage, yoga, deep breathing, etc.—any activity that is stress-free.

Mindfulness

Meditation and mindfulness are considered important today and for good reason. Yogis have been practising *dhyan* (meditation) for ages. It is a practice to quieten our mind and to reduce our everyday stress.

Meditation and Relaxation • 131

How to Meditate: A Simple Meditation Technique for Beginners

1. Sit or lie down in any comfortable position.
2. Close your eyes.
3. Breathe naturally.
4. Focus your attention on each inhalation and exhalation.

Brain scan studies show that meditation can physically alter the structure of the brain so that it no longer feels pain with the same level of intensity.

Benefits of Meditation

- Studies show that meditation dramatically improves your fluid intelligence as well as your overall IQ.
- It reduces overall stress.
- It improves mood.
- Studies have also found that ageing people who meditate regularly lose their gray matter at a slower rate than people who don't.

In 2011, Sara Lazar and her team at Harvard found that mindfulness meditation can actually change the structure of the brain: Eight weeks of Mindfulness-Based Stress Reduction (MBSR) was found to increase cortical thickness in the hippocampus, which governs learning and memory, and in certain areas of the brain.

Zen Buddhism dictates a technique for controlling our mind. It is one of the simplest techniques to follow, which produces profound results. One is required to be *aware* of his thoughts, feelings and actions. One has to live in the present all the time, not reflect on the past or project things into the future with anxiety. When the thoughts and emotions drift into negative and impure aspects, one should *beware* of its implications and thereby change the pattern of one's thoughts and feelings.

Activity

Breathe in and out. While doing so, concentrate on your breath properly. While you inhale, imagine the flow of air passing inside the body and concentrate on the flow. Hold your breath and count from 1 to 10. Then exhale and observe the air flow. Once you exhale, count from 1 to 10 before inhaling, and then repeat the process at least five times when you are free, and feel the difference.

This exercise will sharpen your awareness about the things happening around you and your conscious mind will help you in analysing, thinking and making decisions.

The most important factors for a good memory are the following:

1. Interest, attention and motivation are essential prerequisites for an excellent memory.
2. Thoughts either support you or they don't. Some can be helpful and effective. Others can be limiting, negative and harmful. And a lot of thoughts can be just mental noise; nothing important.
3. There is no limit to the capacity of memory. The more you remember, the more you *can* remember. There is no such thing as bad or good memory. There is only trained and untrained memory.

Note: Practice techniques daily.

Further Benefits of Meditation

- Understanding yourself properly
- Better decision-making process

- Greater awareness of situations
- Becoming more proactive
- Improved thinking process

Relaxation can be achieved through progressive muscle relaxation. Relaxation helps cope with stress. Stress is the leading cause of mental problems and physical issues.

The Life Wheel

Mark the following points on a scale of 0-10 (0-low and 10-high) in the image below. Connect the dots and you will find the diagram showing your Life Wheel.

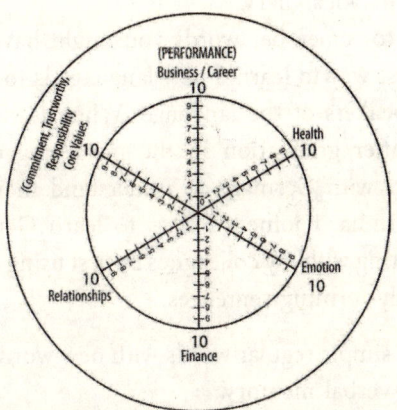

Summary

In this chapter, we have learnt:

- How to meditate
- Benefits of meditation
- How to draw your Life Wheel

Chapter 15

Learning a Foreign Language

Introduction

One of the biggest hurdles in learning a new language is remembering its vocabulary.

You have to remember words you might have never heard before. The best way to learn a new language is to communicate with native speakers of the language. When I was working on my first job after graduation in the marketing department, I had to interact with Germans to understand their product for marketing in India. I joined a class to learn German where I started interacting with my colleagues by first using certain words, and then slowly forming sentences.

TIP: Associate simple regular words with new words and connect them through verbal memory.

Basic Vocabulary Rules

1. When you come across a new word, the first rule is Repeat! Everyone has a different way of learning. If you are a visual learner, then you can first write the word and then draw images and try to connect them with the meanings of the words. If you are an auditory learner, you can learn any

language faster by listening to it being spoken.
2. Write down words and their corresponding meanings and stick them somewhere where you can regularly see them, like your cupboard, study desk, etc.
3. Use them often, in office, at home or while talking on the phone.

Words convey meaning. Words are used as tools to communicate feelings, expressions, messages, etc. The ingredients are mixed in specific proportions and then communicated via a signal. Let's now learn how you can play with the stuff that you wish to understand and reproduce them better.

Vocabulary Creative Technique

Whenever we come across a new word, we need to first learn how to pronounce that word. Phonetics or speech sounds help us to pronounce accurately.

The second step is to try to analyse the word and see if it can be:

Substituted: What other word, either in your mother tongue or in any other known language, can be used instead of what has been used?

Connected: What other words can be connected to the word through phonetic association?

Combined: What else can be combined with it to create something new and remarkable, or easy to remember?

Adjusted: How can you convey the same meaning with more or fewer words?

Absorbed: What can the word absorb to perform a new function?

Magnified: How can you enlarge its scope, i.e, how can you apply your creative skills to make it more visible?

Used: What other use can you think of for it?

Eliminated: What can you eliminate/remove to form a meaningful and understandable word and reduce the clutter?

Reversed: What happens if you turn it upside-down or back-to-front?

Rearranged: How can you reconfigure the constituent words or letters in the given word?

This technique can be used for:

- Learning new words—easy memorization and recall
- Learning any foreign language
- Everyday life
- Identifying comparative words and expressions

Activity

Can you recall and note below the objects you have touched, pictured, smelled or heard, and the equivalent words in the language you are learning from your experience? Differentiate the objects according to the way they feel in the respective boxes.

Soft:	Slimy:	Textured:

TIP: Understand how fast you respond to each stimulus and how they stimulate your senses.

Do you remember the process of creating stories for your brain?

The tips provided in Chapter 4 will be just as helpful when applied to learning a new language!

Activity

Episodic Memory

In the following table, identify the relevant product for each slogan from memory, then mark the kind of sensory memory each slogan triggers:

Visual (V), Auditory (A), Touch (To), Taste (Ts), Smell (S)... Tick ☑ wherever it is applicable.

Sr. No	KEYWORDS/IMAGE/HINT	PRODUCT	V	A	To	Ts	S
1	DAAG ACCHE HAI	SURF	√	√			√
2	ZUBAN PE LAGAAM						
3	MINT WITH A HOLE						
4	MAA NE BANAYE HAI						
5	MAA KI YAAD AA GAI						
6	YOU ARE WORTH IT						
7	TASTE THE THUNDER						
8	DO GHUT KI BAAT HAI						
9	JUST DO IT!						

Activity

Now, let's do a vocabulary activity. We have already learnt the Vocabulary Creative Technique which helps us analyse a new word we are learning.

For example:

Word: Gullible
Phonetics: GULL-uh-bul

Meaning: easily duped or cheated

Substitute	Gulli-Danda (Cricket)
Connect	Gel
Combine	
Adjust	
Absorb	
Magnify	
Use	
Eliminate	
Reverse	
Rearrange	

You can also draw symbols or create a memory image, which can help you to memorize/visualize the word along with its meaning and reproduce it when called for.

The definition of the word can be brought to life via comparison, symbols, links, expressions and memory images.

Now let's follow the same technique for the word below and fill the table:

Word: Fanatic
Phonetics: ———————
Meaning: ————————————————————————

Substitute	
Connect	
Combine	
Adjust	
Absorb	
Magnify	
Use	
Eliminate	
Reverse	
Rearrange	

Flash Cards

You can also use flash cards for each word.

FRONT:

```
SUBSTITUTE                          ADJUST
CONNECT                             ABSORB
COMBINE

              WORLD

MAGNIFY                           ELIMINATE
  USE                              REVERSE
```

BACK

> MEANING

Activity

A few words and their meanings are given below. Associate the words and their meanings to create imaginary stories. Check if this helps you recall the words and their meanings.

Katzenjammer: noun | KAT-sun-jam-er

Meaning: distress, depression or confusion caused by a hangover.

_____
_____
_____

Opusculum: noun | oh-PUSK-yuh-lum
Meaning: a minor work (of literature)—usually used in plural form.

_____
_____
_____

Whenever you need to study a new word either to get the meaning, translate it into another language or to learn a sequence of new words:

1. Write out the new word and its meaning in the following order—word in <FOREIGN LANGUAGE>, pronunciation key and translation into English.
2. Recall images or senses evoked by the word, paying particular attention to a thorough selection of visual images.
3. While memorizing, listen to the pronunciation of the word by a native speaker and repeat it in your mind.
4. Memorize difficult words using similar-sounding words or phonetically similar sounds from a language you are fluent in.
5. Recite words from memory whenever you have spare time.

Sequence Memorization

There is no need to have a lot of support images to memorize a sequence of new foreign words. After the connection between image-sense and word pronunciation is fixed, support images can be used repeatedly.

Let us say that you have memorized fifty new words. Words can be memorized quite fast. Even if you spend a maximum of one minute per new word, you can still memorize about fifty words per hour. This is the actual time required for qualitative memorizing.

The following points are important.

- Do not attempt to learn a song's lyrics in one day. On the first day, you will capture phrases and may be able to deliver it roughly. You will need at least four days to be able to automatically reproduce the lyrics without thinking. During that time the lyrics should be repeated periodically

from memory. The same goes for a group of new words.
- If you need to retell a text on Friday, you need to memorize it on Monday.

To develop a connection between a visual image and a word pronunciation, you need to activate this connection over a couple of days.

Periodically imagine and pronounce a word via a support image. This should be done with all words and only by heart. If you memorized fifty words today then tomorrow you will need to view them in your imagination to form the connection 'between image and pronunciation'.

The next day you will need ten new support images for the memorization of a new group of words.

On the third day, you should memorize ten more new words but continue imagining the first and second groups of words.

On the fourth day, memorize ten more new words but continue imagining the first, second and the third groups of words.

On the fifth day you will be able to memorize new words on the first fifty support images.

NOTE:

You do not have to memorize ten to fifteen new words every day. You can memorize one group of words and repeat it over several days. After strengthening a group of words in your memory, you can memorize the next group. If you memorize twenty new words every three days—you will still learn 200 words per month. Not bad! You can start reading children books. For this you will need fifty to hundred support images.

Choosing Sight Words

A sight word vocabulary is a store of words a student can identify and/or read automatically. They know the words by sight. They do not need to say the words out loud. Sight words should include high frequency words, i.e., words commonly used in everyday conversation and common words you see in print. One of the best sources to find sight words is from the Dolch word list. You can actually get it online for free. Learning these 220 words can help a child read approximately 50 to 75 per cent of what is printed in almost any piece of children's literature.

Making Sight Word Flash Cards

To make sight word flash cards, all you need are index cards.

Activity

Add and Replace:
  Either delete, replace, or add one letter in each of the following words in order to arrive at a new, meaningful word. Start with the first letter. One example is provided for you.

MAID (Example)	Raid	Rain	Ran	Rin	
BUN					
SOUTH					
INVERT					
POST					
FINE					
FIX					
DEAR					
CRACK					

MATE					
PLANE					
ROSE					
PINE					

Improve Your Memory

Learning a foreign language is a good method that one can use to practise techniques to improve one's memory. Learning a new set of words is often a matter of associating nonsensical set of syllables with counterparts in your own language.

Normally, most people memorize foreign words by repeating them over and over again. You can improve this laborious way of learning by using two main techniques:

1. **Use Mnemonics**

    This is a very simple way of using the association method. You can use images or other simple methods to link words or phrases in your own language their counterpart in the foreign one.

    For example, in learning English-Spanish vocabulary:

    English: apple—Spanish: manzana. You can associate the last letter of manzana to the first letter of the word apple.

    English: olives—Spanish: oliva. Just eliminate the last letter and pronounce it as olive.

2. **The Town Language Mnemonic**

    This technique is based on the fact that the regular vocabulary of a language relates to common things—things that you may, say, normally find in a town. In using this technique, choose a place that you know. You can use objects within the town as cues to remember images that relate to the foreign vocabulary.

For example, in learning nouns, you can associate common words to the most relevant locations. You can relate the word for a book with an image of a library. Words for fruits can be associated to a fruit stand. The names for different vegetables can be associated with the market.

In learning adjectives, you can relate common words to things found in, say, gardens or parks. Words such as green, fragrant, dark, large, hot, etc. can be easily associated with common objects in the park. You can also imagine a public pool or a pond, or even people, and describe what you see.

If you want to learn verbs, associate with a gym or a sports centre. Most activities in the sports centre can be associated with the foreign words for walking, dancing, jumping, swimming, etc.

If you are learning a language where gender is important, an effective method to recall it is by dividing objects in a town into two main categories. In one group you can group objects coded as male, while in the other group you can associate do so for the female gender. If the language has other genders, then associate the proper groups. You can associate these divisions with roads, ponds, lakes, rivers, etc.

Another easy way of remembering foreign words is to memorize the hundred most common words in a language. Just select the most important words that you need to learn.

Summary

In this chapter, we have learnt:

- Basic vocabulary rules
- Vocabulary Creative Technique
- Ways of learning a new language

Chapter 16

Tackling Memory Disorders

Introduction

Alzheimer's is a type of dementia that causes problems with memory, thinking and behaviour. Symptoms usually develop slowly and get worse over time, becoming severe enough to interfere with daily tasks.

Most professionals are now tech-savvy and hardly use their complete brain potential in handling even simple tasks such as calculating, determining a date or even recalling regularly used contact numbers. We are all completely dependent on smart devices, which I call 'dumb babies' since they cannot do anything on their own. By using this external source, we are neglecting the mental powers that we developed and nurtured as children. It is estimated that in the future, machines will take over the jobs of humans and we may have to face an unemployment crisis. It's time that we wake up and work on our brain powers and make them stronger. Due to our lifestyles in our urban world, we are increasingly in danger of suffering from mental disorders. This chapter shall explain how you can deal with mental disorders and lead a happy life.

Reasons for Memory Loss

Transience: Memories are disconnected with the passing of time.

Memories are lost slowly, unknowingly. This occurs in the primary stage of storage, after the information has been stored but before it is retrieved. This can happen in sensory, short-term and long-term storage. It follows a certain pattern where the information is rapidly forgotten in spite of trying to recall it from memory, followed by small losses in later days.

Absentmindedness: Uncertainty or memory loss due to the lack of proper attention. This happens because of involvement in multitasking activities and lack of a proper attention span. Multiple thought processes hinder the mind from focusing on the main area of concentration. Repeating such behaviour leads to absentmindedness.

Ageing: One of the key concerns of older adults is the experience of memory loss. However, memory loss is qualitatively different in normal ageing from the kind of memory loss associated with a diagnosis of Alzheimer's. Ageing can be controlled by performing certain daily simple exercises.

The Stages of Alzheimer's

First stage:

The person is mentally healthy. It forms the base to which all other stages are compared.

Second stage:

Age-related forgetfulness: Generally, over the age of sixty-five, people start experiencing symptoms of forgetfulness much before they enter into the old age bracket. They suffer from an inability to recall

- Names of people they just met
- Where they kept specific things
- The right word or information at the right time

These common symptoms are initially not noticed, or even ignored by many.

Third stage:

Mild Cognitive Impairment: As the second stage symptoms become more prominent and are even noticed by family members, the affected individual is not even able to perform routine tasks. At this stage the person finds it difficult to concentrate, since their memory has been adversely affected. During this stage, it is said that dementia sets in. As the damage spreads, cells lose their ability to do their jobs and eventually die, causing irreversible changes in the brain.

Fourth stage:

Mild symptoms of Alzheimer's: here the symptoms are clearly noticeable. The person, affected by dementia, even forgets major events of the recent past like:

- A holiday with the family,
- Guests at a recently attended function,
- A visit to a relative's or a friend's place,
- The day of the week or the month,
- Even small activities that are performed on a regular basis

Please note that somehow people can manage themselves at this stage, but the awareness that they are losing their ability to perform certain tasks and admitting the decline is a challenge for people.

Fifth stage:

Moderate symptoms of Alzheimer's: This stage is often called the first real stage of an Alzheimer patient. At this stage the affected person can no longer manage things independently, and faces more difficulties in their day to day activities.

They can forget old memories like:

- year of graduation,
- first job,
- family events in the past,
- marriage, and
- even one's own address.

Sixth stage:

Moderately severe Alzheimer's: At this stage there is increasing decline in the ability of an affected person to perform basic tasks such as:

- putting on clothes properly,
- taking a bath,
- eating food,
- recognizing even close relatives.

In addition, speech may become slurred—a symptom characterized by poor pronunciation of words, mumbling, or a change in speed or rhythm while talking. The medical term for slurred speech is dysarthria. Slurred speech may develop slowly over time, or following a single incident.

Seventh stage:

Severe Alzheimer's disease: This is the last stage. At this stage the patient requires assistance in all the basic daily activities, and help with physical movement.

At this stage the person becomes totally dependent and starts deteriorating day by day.

Whenever you feel that there is a change in your behaviour, habits and regular movements, or are getting frequent mood swings, you should visit a good neurophysician right in the beginning, rather than avoiding or shuffling between physicians, psychologists and psychiatrists or counsellors. There is no doubt about the positive effects of a proper early diagnosis and treatment. The bitter truth about the disease is that it has *no cure* and that with every passing year, it becomes worse.

Prevention of Alzheimer's and Dementia

By identifying and controlling your personal habits and behaviour patterns, you can maximize your chances of lifelong brain health and take active steps to preserve your cognitive abilities (cognition mainly refers to memory, speech, the ability to learn new information and understanding and comprehending written material or available information).

Cognitive skills are the core skills your brain uses to:

- think,
- read,
- learn,
- remember,
- reason,
- pay attention.

Six Tools of Alzheimer's Prevention

With regular practice and utilization of the tools below, your brain will stay active and chances of developing dementia will be drastically reduced.

Tool #1: Regular exercise

According to the Alzheimer's Research and Prevention Foundation, regular physical exercise can reduce your risk of developing Alzheimer's by *up to 50 per cent*.

Activity

- Start morning walk on daily basis
- Swimming
- Moderate weight and resistance training
- Yoga (balance and co-ordination exercises)

Tool #2: Healthy diet

By adjusting your eating habits you can reduce chances of Alzheimer's and protect your brain from unhealthy and junk food.

Have plenty of Omega-3 fats: walnuts, kidney beans, soybean oil, chia seeds, etc. For non-vegetarians, cold-water fish such as salmon, tuna, trout, mackerel, and sardines as well as seaweed are beneficial. You can also supplement these with fish oil.

Have lots of green leafy vegetables, berries and cruciferous vegetables such as broccoli.

Regular consumption of green tea may enhance memory and mental alertness and slow brain ageing.

Home food ensures that you are eating fresh, and consuming more healthy nutrients.

Tool #3: Mental health and hygiene

Be in the company of learners. Those who continue learning new things every day and challenge their brains throughout their lives are less likely to develop Alzheimer's disease and dementia.

Activities

- Join a library.
- Subscribe to educational YouTube channels.
- Read newspapers or good books.
- Write poems or stories.
- Join a foreign language course.
- Learn a musical instrument.
- Learn to paint.

Tool #4: Mental energy

Activate your brain cells by feeding them with energizers.

Activity

Practice memorization

Use the techniques learnt in Chapters 5 and 8.

Memorize Pi digits:

3.1415926535 8979323846 2643383279 5028841971 6939937510
5820974944 5923078164 0628620899 8628034825 3421170679

Now cover the above digits and check if you can recall the same.

Enjoy strategy games, puzzles and riddles:

Solve a crossword puzzle or a number puzzle like Sudoku, play board games or word games like Scrabble, or learn and use a new word every day.

Practise the five Ws:

Keep a 'Who, What, Where, When and Why' list of your daily experiences.

Imagine the following scenarios.

'What if' you are selected for the post of the prime minister?

'How' can you change your work environment?

'Who' would you like your boss to be?

'Where' do you like to go on your dream vacation?

_____
_____
_____
_____

Tool #5: Social interaction and networking

Instead of connecting and liking messages, jokes, events and conveying your feelings through emoji images, have a face-to-face meeting with your friends and relatives who care for you. Staying socially engaged protects against Alzheimer's and dementia, so develop and maintain a strong network and interact with like-minded people. Be in the company of intellectuals, be it in sports, politics or social events.

Activity

- Volunteer for any activity.
- Join a club or a social group.
- Take group classes—art, painting, etc.
- Interact with friends and relatives over phone or e-mail.
- Connect with new friends and search for old ones via social networking sites.
- Network with your neighbours.
- Go to the movies or visit the park, museums and other public places.

Tool #6: Good sleep

New research suggests that disrupted sleep isn't just a symptom of Alzheimer's, but a possible risk factor. An increasing number of studies have linked poor sleep with interference in memory formation, slowing down your thinking, affecting your mood and other behaviourial changes. Deep and sound sleep is necessary. Going to bed and getting up at regular times reinforces your natural circadian rhythms. Your brain's clock responds to regularity.

Regular Activities

Set a mood: Reserve your time for bed and ban television and any technological gadgets from the bedroom.

Bedtime ritual: Take a hot shower and dim the lights while sleeping. This will send a powerful signal to your brain cells that it's time for sleep.

Take short naps: Short naps are a great way to recharge your neurons. Do it during early afternoon and limit it to twenty to thirty minutes.

Remove stress/anxiety: If you are stressed or have anxiety or are not in a good mood, just get out of bed. Try reading or just relaxing or taking a shower, and then get back to bed.

Other Tips to Prevent Alzheimer's

Stop smoking: One study found that smokers over the age of 65 have a nearly 80 per cent higher risk of Alzheimer's than those who have never smoked. Non-smokers benefit from better circulation.

Control blood pressure and cholesterol levels: Both high blood pressure and high total cholesterol creates a high risk of Alzheimer's disease. Controlling these numbers are good for your brain as well as your heart.

Drinking habits: Heavy alcohol consumption can dramatically raise the risk of Alzheimer's and accelerate brain ageing.

Summary

In this chapter, we have learnt:

- What Alzheimer's disease is
- Stages of Alzheimer's
- Prevention of Alzheimer's and dementia

Acknowledgements

Special thanks to my corporate business associates, and the entrepreneurs who inspired and motivated me to share the knowledge and learnings I have acquired in my journey of over twenty years. My wife Madhuri and my two sons Chinmai and Soham have been solid sources of inspiration and support, both morally and spiritually, in writing this book.

I am also thankful to my relatives, my partners and my associates, who have all been a part of my successful journey. I would also like to extend my gratitude to the following (in alphabetical order)—Ajay Darekar, Ameena Yusuf (Egypt), Anand Kulkarni, Angela (SA), Aishwarya Atre, Anil Kumar, Anita Gosal, Anuja Salwatkar, Arun Chitlangia, Arvind Gawade, Ashitosh Kulkarni, Besant School Teachers, Bhagyashree Dange, Bhupesh Dange, Chaaya Todankar, Chanda Surve, Daksha Chitrodia, Devendra Madan, Devina Adhiya, Dilip Patil, Dilip Tikle, Dilip Mukerjea (Singapore), Dipti Kulkarni, Edna Periera (UAE), Fenil Shah, Francis Xaviers, Gargi Lagoo, Gaurav Bhandari, Ganesh Tendulkar, Ghanshyam Deshpande, Hemant Joshi, (Bahrain), Hemant Deodhar, Indranil Mayekar, Jigish Bhatt, Jitendra Ahirkar, Jitendra Mali, Jyoti Vora, Kavita Kanojia, Kiranpal Singh Chawla, Kranthiraj, Lata Joshi, Lesley Gosling (USA), Madan Panse, Madhura Panse, Mahesh Golani, Manish Phadke, Manisha Dopeshwar, Mirendra Shahare, Mohan Panse, Mohammed Shalaby (Kuwait), N.L. Shraman, Namrata Thakker, Neha Davda, Nilay Vaidya, Nishigandha Kalyankar, Niti Tayal, Nitin Mendosa,

Nitin Patil, Nitin Poddar, Niyati Shah, Nitin Xerox, Omkar kibe, Omprakash Sahu, Pawan Agrawal, Prashant Gundawar, Prateek Yadav, Pritam Gade (UAE), Rajesh Tayal, Ravikant Iyer, Ripu Ranjan Sinha, Ritesh (UAE), Rushikesh Borde, Sameer Rane, Sandeep kulkarni (UAE), Sandeep Sarang, Santosh Pawar, Santosh Bhagat, Saraswathi Bhamidi, Shantala Panse, Shrikant Raje, Smita Deo, Snehal Panse, Subhash Jain, Suraj Lokare, Suresh Kukreja, Vikrant Chaphekar, Vishwajeet Suvarna, Winston Jacob and Zenobia Ba.

I would also like to thank the Rupa team for their support.